Y0-DRV-357

**THIS BOOKLET IS NOT TO BE SOLD.**
It is a free educational service in the public interest, published by the Philadelphia Church of God.

© 2016, 2017 Philadelphia Church of God
All Rights Reserved

Printed in the United States of America

Scriptures in this publication are quoted from the King James Version, unless otherwise noted.

Cover image: iStock.com/uschools

# GREAT AGAIN

## WHY AMERICA IS FALLING FAST—BUT ITS GREATEST GLORY EVER IS IMMINENT

GERALD FLURRY

# CONTENTS

INTRODUCTION

# Make America Great Again?

DO YOU BELIEVE THE UNITED STATES OF AMERICA HAS been mainly a positive force in the world for most of its history?

Do you have a favorable view of the Founding Fathers, the Constitution, separation of powers, rule of law, Manifest Destiny, freedom of religion, freedom of speech, free-market economy, and America's role in World Wars I and II?

IF YOU DO, THEN SURELY YOU ARE DEEPLY ALARMED BY THE STATE OF AMERICA TODAY.

*All* of these pillars of American history and identity are being vilified and destroyed. America's educators are teaching oncoming generations to be *embarrassed* by them. Even the nation's leaders see them as shameful. On many foundational issues, they share the views of America's worst enemies!

The nation's foreign policy is utterly transformed. We have seen apologies, concessions and surrenders made to dictators and despots, while longtime alliances, like those with the United Kingdom and the Jewish state of Israel, have been cast aside. Nations that have relied on America for leadership, strength, security, protection and largesse face a new reality and are having to forge alternate relationships, even if they undermine America.

THERE IS A SPIRITUAL DIMENSION TO AMERICA'S DECLINE THAT MOST PEOPLE DO NOT SEE. The crisis facing this nation is *not* because of a bad president! THE CAUSE IS FAR DEEPER. But most people are unwilling to face it.

Many Americans realize that the nation is off track and suffering. You hear a lot of people speaking out about what ails America and how to fix it.

On one side of the political spectrum are people who are upset about many things—but who believe America's problems are a result of *its past.* They think the nation hasn't departed *far enough* from its founding principles of limited government, individual liberty and free markets. Unlike the founders, they believe the federal government should be larger and more powerful. That it should claim more of people's income and redistribute it to those it deems deserving. That rather than safeguarding equal opportunity, it should impose and enforce equal outcomes. They believe America should be *more* like some of the worst failed governmental experiments in human history!

The fact that these views have such a large and fanatical following speaks volumes about how radically different the United States is today from what it was even one or two generations ago! You can read more about where these ideas originated and why they have become so popular in Chapter 3 of this booklet.

A lot of Americans are upset and anxious about America's direction—but tend to view the biggest problems as *more recent*. These people believe that the nation's economy, military, diplomacy and global influence have gotten dangerously weak. They see trends like anti-American political correctness and rampant illegal immigration as being threats to the country. They see that America is in trouble, and they want solutions.

Donald Trump's presidential campaign in 2016 captured the support of this segment of Americans. Mr. Trump does an admirable job of identifying these problems and addressing people's concerns. His slogan is "Make America Great Again."

That slogan resonates with a lot of people who believe the United States has been mainly a positive force in the world—people who are not embarrassed by the nation's history and unique identity.

Anyone who sincerely admires this country wants to see America made great again.

The Bible has a lot to say about the state of America today. It explains the inspiring reason *why* this nation was so great in the first place. And why it has been so richly blessed.

THE BIBLE ALSO *PROPHESIES* THAT THESE BLESSINGS WOULD BE *REMOVED* IN OUR DAY. AMERICA'S PROBLEMS ARE SPIRITUAL—AND SOLVING THEM REQUIRES SPIRITUAL SOLUTIONS.

Could Mr. Trump's presidency be prophesied in your Bible?

I'm going to explain some *revealed* truth to you that should electrify every American. And it will in time. That also includes every person on this planet.

What you read in this booklet can be *proved*—every chapter. The first chapter reveals some of the greatest fulfilled prophecy ever from God's inspired Bible.

If you keep an open mind, it could galvanize your life as nothing ever has before!

If you have living faith in this message, it will give you the most majestic reward offered in the Bible.

ONE

# Who Is the Modern-Day Jeroboam?

DONALD TRUMP'S VICTORY IN THE UNITED STATES presidential election gives us a clear indication as to where we are in Bible prophecy.

Most people pay little attention to Bible prophecy. But did you know that ONE THIRD of the Bible is prophecy, and 90 percent of that prophecy is for our day?

In the weeks before the election, Hillary Clinton held a considerable lead in the polls. But in a sermon at the same time, I commented that I was leaning toward Mr. Trump being the winner. Why? Because of an end-time prophecy in the book of Amos.

The Prophet Amos recorded a prophecy about a

leader named Jeroboam. I want to show you that this is referring to a powerful individual who is on the scene right now.

You can't fully understand the Amos prophecy without knowing *who* Jeroboam is. You desperately need to understand why God is revealing names in this book!

It seems obvious that God is telling us we have now entered the time frame of Amos chapter 7. What does that time frame mean for America and for YOU? God has REVEALED to me more understanding from Amos 7.

The book of Amos has some of the strongest prophecies in the Bible, with little emphasis on the positive message. But there is great hope in this prophetic book.

## The Time of Jeroboam

The prophecy of Amos 7 is directed specifically at "Israel" (see verse 8). Although the Jewish state in the Middle East took that name when it formed in 1948, when Israel is used in prophecy it has a wider meaning. It is referring to the modern nations descended from the 12 tribes of the biblical nation of Israel. This is a foundational truth that you must prove in order to understand the Bible's prophecies. It is explained in exciting detail in Herbert W. Armstrong's book *The United States and Britain in Prophecy*, a book that we will gladly send you free upon request.

Look now at the specifics of this prophecy of Amos: "Thus he shewed me: and, behold, the Lord stood upon a wall made by a plumbline, with a plumbline in his hand" (verse 7). A plumbline is usually used in measuring a building or in construction. But God uses it differently here: This is about measuring the *destruction* that is to come upon the nations of Israel. THIS DESTRUCTION

IS NOT RANDOM; GOD IS MEASURING IT CAREFULLY AND PRECISELY. And it will bring about the most wonderful results imaginable.

"And the LORD said unto me, Amos, what seest thou? And I said, A plumbline. Then said the Lord, Behold, I will set a plumbline in the midst of my people Israel: *I will not again pass by them any more*" (verse 8). This is GOD speaking! In recent years, He has warned these nations many times to try to wake them up, but they have ignored these warnings. So, He says, *I'll warn one last time.* He is giving these people one last chance to repent!

We are entering the *last time* that God passes by the people of Israel before they are destroyed! This is a time of extreme urgency!

And notice: THIS IS IN THE CONTEXT OF AN END-TIME *JEROBOAM.* Verse 9 continues: "And the high places of Isaac shall be desolate, and the sanctuaries of Israel shall be laid waste; and I will rise against THE HOUSE OF JEROBOAM with the sword."

When God says, "I will not again pass by them any more," He is talking about them being destroyed in the *time of Jeroboam.*

Who is Jeroboam? Who is this *specific man* that Amos prophesies will be ruling the superpower of Israel when the final warning ends? There are two nations that prophetically have the name of biblical Israel in this end time—Britain and the superpower America.

God is telling the end-time nations of Israel how to solve their problems and difficulties, and to warn them of the consequences of their failure to do so.

This chapter states that God is going to rise with the sword against them *in the time of Jeroboam.* The Moffatt translation renders the end of verse 9 as, "I will attack

Jeroboam's house." There is something very upsetting to God about the house of Jeroboam. This is why He wants us to understand it and why it is so *offensive* to Him!

God emphasizes the U.S. superpower, the leader of the nations of Israel. The U.S. is led by a modern-day Jeroboam. When there is a type of Jeroboam on the scene, then God will send the sword upon His people because of all of their sins. It is because of AMERICA'S SINS that it must suffer!

This is sobering to think about. Here is a severe end-time prophecy, and GOD IS SPEAKING ABOUT AN INDIVIDUAL. God *names names!* WE MUST UNDERSTAND THESE NAMES AND THE ROLES THESE MEN PLAY IF WE ARE TO UNDERSTAND THESE END-TIME PROPHECIES! It is *essential* that we know who these individuals are.

God gives us checkpoints in Bible prophecy: the "time of the end" (e.g. Daniel 12:4), the "last end" (Daniel 8:19), and the "last HOUR" (1 John 2:18; Revised Standard Version; request my free booklet *The Last Hour* for an explanation). This prophecy occurs in the *Jeroboam time frame*—or, we could say, the JEROBOAM END—the LAST TIME God will pass by with His message! God will not bring this warning to His people again; the Jeroboam time is going to be the LAST TIME!

If you understand this, it really makes Bible prophecy come alive to you. God is revealing the identity of *significant* individuals in Bible prophecy in this end time especially—I believe like He's never done before. He wants us to understand this because it is leading directly into the Great Tribulation and then the coming of the Messiah! Though it is extremely distressing news in the short run, what it leads to is THE GREATEST NEWS YOU COULD HEAR!

## The Land Cannot Bear His Words

Amos's prophecy continues: "Then Amaziah the priest of Bethel sent to Jeroboam king of Israel, saying, Amos hath conspired against thee in the midst of the house of Israel: THE LAND IS NOT ABLE TO BEAR ALL HIS WORDS" (Amos 7:10).

God is sending His message into the "MIDST of the house of Israel," into the very heart of America and Britain. The Philadelphia Church of God message is going to take center stage.

Just watch how this prophecy is going to be fulfilled.

GOD HAS SPOKEN!

It is OUR WORDS that the land will not be able to bear! This strongly indicates that there are SERIOUS PROBLEMS plaguing the nation or they wouldn't care what we say. But we have a message they cannot bear because IT IS ABOUT THEIR DESTRUCTION—AT A TIME WHEN THEIR PROBLEMS ARE SOARING! Most people want to close their minds to what is coming upon them—instead of repenting of their sins.

Who is this "priest of Bethel"? "Bethel" means *house of God.* "Amaziah the priest of Bethel" is prophetic language referring to a man who came from *within the Church of God* in this end time. You can see from the prophecy in Revelation 3 beginning in verse 14 that the *last era* of God's true Church before Christ's return—the very time frame we are in right now—is the *Laodicean* era, a lukewarm church that has turned its back on God. *Amaziah* is a very rebellious Laodicean minister.

*Here Amaziah is accusing Amos, God's true prophet, of treason—"conspiring against" Jeroboam!* Amos is a type of the man in this end time who is proclaiming God's warning message to Israel today. So this is a prophecy of a real clash between a false minister and a true prophet of God.

I believe Amaziah the priest is the same man as the leader of God's rebellious Church whom we battled with for copyrights to the truth and message of God (Amos 9:1, 11-12). Amaziah HATES our message. He is almost certainly the individual who led a six-year court battle trying to suppress God's truth from going out to this world! (You can read more about that Amos 9 court battle in our free booklet *The Lion Has Roared.*) Satan doesn't like that we won that battle and made him look bad. He never gives up when something like that happens. We are in the middle of Satan's worst wrath.

The priest Amaziah is sending this message about Amos to Jeroboam. This strongly indicates that the end-time Jeroboam has a RELIGIOUS following! He is leading people further away from God.

Look again at Amos 7:9, and you see more religious imagery. As our booklet on Amos, *The Lion Has Roared*, explains, "the high places of Isaac" refers to the Laodicean Church. The "sanctuaries of Israel" are the religions of this world, like the evangelicals.

Mr. Trump received over 80 percent of the white evangelical vote and a large portion of the Catholic vote. He really is leading most of America's "religious" people. BUT WHERE IS HE LEADING THEM?

This is quite different religiously from what you find in Britain—the other birthright nation. Jeroboam is leading the superpower of Israel.

## 'Thus Saith the Lord'

Amaziah's message to Jeroboam is, "The land is not able to bear all his words." What "words" are so difficult to bear? Amaziah explains: "For thus AMOS SAITH, JEROBOAM SHALL DIE BY THE SWORD, and Israel shall surely be led away captive out of their own land" (Amos 7:11).

In the short run, this *is* bad news. But it is a message from God that MUST BE DELIVERED! This false priest will go before Jeroboam and say, "This is what AMOS says." He doesn't say that this is a message FROM GOD! But when Amos speaks, he says, "[H]ear thou the word of the LORD .... [T]hus saith the LORD"! (verses 16-17). AMOS CAME WITH A "THUS SAITH THE LORD" MESSAGE! Amos is just the messenger. God gives the messenger His message and says, *Go and deliver this to my people.*

The world doesn't want to believe this is from God. They almost always look at it as a message from a man. But it isn't! THIS IS WHAT *GOD* SAYS! It's such a powerful message that you cannot deny it is coming from God—but the world still tries.

We all have human nature, but we must overcome it or we too will think, *Well that's just a man's opinion; I don't think it is from God.* WE HAVE TO STAY FOCUSED ON "THUS SAITH THE LORD"! THIS IS A MESSAGE FROM GOD!

America has different messages coming from Republicans and Democrats, but THE ONLY MESSAGE THAT WILL PREVAIL IS "THUS SAITH THE LORD"! NOTHING ELSE WILL SUCCEED. This world must understand that.

How well do YOU understand that God is sending out HIS WORD today? The message you are reading right now is coming from *His mouth.* And you can prove it. This is critical understanding that ought to sober anybody!

For decades, this Work has been warning America and Britain about what is going to happen, but people have scorned this message and pushed it aside. Yet there will come a point when people cannot bear it anymore.

Still, the message is wrapped in wonderful good news. Even though there is bad news in the short term, THIS IS

THE BEGINNING OF ISRAEL GETTING TO KNOW GOD! There will be rough times ahead, but God is going to use those trials to help Israel get to know Him! We have to see the destruction in the context of God's plan. This VISION will keep us positive. When you think about the end result, what could be more inspiring?

AT THE TIME OF THE END, JEROBOAM IS GOING TO BE LADEN WITH PROBLEMS AND DIFFICULTIES, BUT HIS BIGGEST PROBLEM IS GOING TO BE THE MESSAGE OF GOD COMING OUT OF THIS ORGANIZATION! Our message is going to plague him! This is what people in this land are going to fear most of all. God is forcing them to face *the warning message* of their own destruction! This is a problem Jeroboam never saw coming.

This modern-day Jeroboam has made it clear that he knows little or nothing about the Bible, which is Jesus Christ in print.

## The King's Chapel

Here is what Herbert W. Armstrong wrote in his book *Mystery of the Ages:* "David's son Solomon became the wisest man who ever lived (except Christ). But he taxed the people very heavily, and when he died his son Rehoboam became king. The people sent a delegation with an ultimatum to Rehoboam. If he would reduce their taxes, they would serve him. If not, they would reject him as king. On the advice of the younger men among his councilors, Rehoboam told the people he would lay even heavier taxes on them.

"Thereupon the people decided against the royal house of David. They named as king, Jeroboam, who had occupied the office we would today call prime minister, under King Solomon. Since Rehoboam was seated on the throne in Jerusalem, the people of Israel chose a new capital some distance north of Jerusalem. (Under a later king, Omri, they built a new northern capital at Samaria.)"

Jeroboam was "a mighty man of valour" and "industrious" (1 Kings 11:28). But he ended up being a disaster for Israel, turning the people away from God by institutionalizing false religion (1 Kings 12). The emphasis in Amos 7 on the "house of Jeroboam" could mean the leader of America in the end time is a physical *descendant* of the original Jeroboam.

It seems logical that God would have an Israelite leader, a Jeroboam type whose ancestors were from ancient Israel, in this end time because our message is to warn Israel, or specifically modern-day America, Britain and the Jewish nation. We have to warn people that it is *their sins* that God is concerned about! There are Gentiles in this land, and they will suffer along with Israel. But God puts the blame on Israel, the house of Jeroboam. That is where the sword is aimed. You probably wouldn't have an Antiochus, a Gentile leader, in office when God is punishing and destroying the house of Jeroboam.

America is one of the *birthright* nations of Israel. God has blessed this land abundantly. Perhaps America's greatest sin is ingratitude to God for making America great!

America's president says, "*I* will make America great again." Notice *the big I: I will make America great again*—not God—*like I made myself great.* That attitude is going to usher in the ultimate disaster. Men vainly think they can do magnificent things. That is one of the most deceitful thoughts anyone can have—especially when you are facing the worst disaster ever! Yet that is what we are facing in this time of Jeroboam.

America, the British peoples (including Canada, Australia, New Zealand and South Africa) and the Jewish nation are facing horrendous problems. ONLY GOD CAN SAVE THESE NATIONS.

For God to save them, our people must repent. Do you see evidence of that happening? I do not. WE NEED A LEADER WHO WILL CAUSE OUR PEOPLE TO EMBRACE THE LIVING GOD—NOT A PUNY, HELPLESS MAN!

THIS MODERN-DAY JEROBOAM FIGHTS FOR MANY GOOD CAUSES. BUT IN THE PROCESS HE GETS PEOPLE TO LOOK TO HIM AS THE SOLUTION—NOT THE OMNIPOTENT, ALL-POWERFUL GOD!

This is the great deception and the great sin.

"Also Amaziah said unto Amos, O thou seer, go, flee thee away into the land of Judah, and there eat bread, and prophesy there: But prophesy not again any more at Bethel: for it is the king's chapel, and it is the king's court" (Amos 7:12-13). Amaziah is being directed by Jeroboam about what to say. He's saying, *Tell them to get out of here! This is "the king's chapel," the president's domain—this is* OUR *religious place. Get out of this land because we will have none of that message!*

This man becomes the evil "Jeroboam" because he is fighting against the message of God—along with Amaziah the priest, who is a spiritual Antiochus. (For more information, request our free booklet *Daniel—Unsealed at Last!*) The modern-day Jeroboam commits the same sin that Jeroboam did anciently. There is a *reason* God uses *Jeroboam* as the last warning to the nations of Israel. The original Jeroboam committed a great sin, and the modern-day Jeroboam is committing the identical sin again. What is that specific sin?

## What Was Jeroboam's Sin?

The book of 1 Kings is part of what is called the former prophets, and it is prophecy mainly for this end time. (Request a free copy of my book *The Former Prophets—How to Become a King.* It explains thoroughly how relevant these biblical books are for us in this end time.)

Notice what Jeroboam did after he received rulership of the 10 northern tribes of Israel: "Then Jeroboam built Shechem in mount Ephraim, and dwelt therein; and went out from thence, and built Penuel. And Jeroboam said in his heart, Now shall the kingdom return to the house of David" (1 Kings 12:25-26). HE FEARED THAT THE PEOPLE WOULD RETURN TO THE HOUSE OF DAVID. THEY HAD JUST BROKEN AWAY, AND HE WANTED TO KEEP THEM SEPARATED FROM KING DAVID'S THRONE. God had even explained the importance of the house of David to Jeroboam (read 1 Kings 11:29-39), but he rejected God's instruction.

Jeroboam wanted to keep the 10 tribes of Israel away from the house of David, denying the eternal promise that God had made to David. So what did he do?

"If this people go up to do sacrifice in the house of the LORD at Jerusalem, then shall the heart of this people turn again unto their lord, even unto Rehoboam king of Judah [Solomon's son], and they shall kill me, and go again to Rehoboam king of Judah. Whereupon the king took counsel, and made two calves of gold, and said unto them, It is too much for you to go up to Jerusalem: behold thy gods, O Israel, which brought thee up out of the land of Egypt" (1 Kings 12:27-28). *Jeroboam took them right back to the false gods they had worshiped shortly after they came out of Egypt and rebelled against God and Moses* (Exodus 32).

Jeroboam then polluted the priesthood by ordaining

priests from "the lowest of the people, which were not of the sons of Levi" (1 Kings 12:31). Then he changed the dates of God's sacred holy days so they would be different from what they were under David and in Jerusalem (verses 32-33). He had his own holy day plan—his own "master plan." HE RIGGED THE SYSTEM SO HE COULD LEAD THE PEOPLE AND KEEP THEM AWAY FROM THE HOUSE OF DAVID. THAT WAS HIS GREAT SIN.

Sadly, the people just went along. They turned away from God and worshiped these golden calves just as they had done in ancient history. This culminated in terrible disaster!

This same sin is being committed today! This is not that difficult to understand or prove: Something is WRONG with most religions today—even those that claim to follow the Bible and to understand God. THE MODERN-DAY JEROBOAM IS CAUSING RELIGIONS TO LOOK TO HIM—not the true God, the only solution to our many destructive problems. It is going the same way it did anciently, only in this end time there is a much greater abundance of truth.

How can we make sure we don't commit this sin?

## The Key of David

We need to view this spiritually, as God does. *You* need to understand the importance of David's throne! This has deep meaning physically and spiritually. I explain it in detail in my book *The Key of David,* which we will send you upon request at no charge.

Revelation 3 beginning in verse 7 describes the *second-to-last* era of God's Church—the one before the Laodicean era. And that message begins: "And to the angel of the church in Philadelphia write; These things saith he that is holy, he that is true, HE THAT HATH THE KEY OF DAVID ...." Jesus Christ has the "key of David," and He gave it to the Philadelphia era of the Church.

Do you hear religions today talking about the key of David? How many traditional Christians, who say they believe the Bible, do you know who talk about and understand the key of David? It seems *strange* to them! The key of David is about a lot more than a man. It is the most important message in the Bible! This is the key that EXPLAINS *the house of David.* It is the ULTIMATE, ALL-INCLUSIVE MESSAGE—the ONLY message—that Christ gave to His Church in this end time—yet most people reject it, just like Jeroboam did. Isn't that amazing? They are following the spirit of Jeroboam!

Herbert W. Armstrong was the leader of God's Church during the Philadelphia era, and he had this key. The Philadelphia Church of God has remained loyal to God in the Laodicean era, and we have clung tightly to this key! The name of our television program is *The Key of David.* We have produced abundant material on the promises God made to David.

In Revelation 3:7, God says that for those who have this *key,* He will OPEN DOORS so they can deliver this message! We must get this: The key of David is the very heart and core of God's message today and throughout most Bible history! But the Jeroboams keep rejecting it. They want to devise their own plans and live by their own rules. That leads to one catastrophe after another after another!

Notice this promise God makes to His faithful Philadelphians: "Because thou hast kept the word of my patience, I also will keep thee from the hour of temptation, which shall come upon all the world, to try them that dwell upon the earth" (verse 10). A GRIEVOUS TRIAL is about to come upon this whole world! Nuclear weapons are proliferating, and they are going to be *used!* But to those who keep the key of David and promote it and teach it and have a work that delivers it, God promises PROTECTION!

Read God's promise to David in 2 Samuel 7:12-13. This is in the former prophets and is also prophecy for today: "And when thy days be fulfilled, and thou shalt sleep with thy fathers, I will set up thy seed after thee, which shall proceed out of thy bowels, and I will establish his kingdom. He shall build an house for my name, and I WILL STABLISH THE THRONE OF HIS KINGDOM FOR EVER." This is an ETERNAL promise!

"And thine house [the house of David] and thy kingdom shall be established for ever before thee: THY THRONE SHALL BE ESTABLISHED FOR EVER" (verse 16). That physical throne still exists today. This wonderful, inspiring message is all explained in *The United States and Britain in Prophecy.* However, this promise from God is really talking about much more than the royal line of a mortal man: It is actually talking about THE THRONE OF GOD! This is God's throne, and He is going to rule from this throne for ALL ETERNITY!

God is inviting human beings to share this throne with Him! If they will be loyal to Him and teach the key of David message, then He will give them the reward of being the Bride of Christ forever—an unparalleled offer to any human being! What a reward God gives those who are loyal to Him before Christ's Second Coming!

THIS IS WHAT JEROBOAM REJECTED. AND A MODERN-DAY JEROBOAM IS GOING TO TURN ISRAEL AWAY FROM THE MESSAGE OF GOD AND THE THRONE OF DAVID.

HE IS OPPOSING *SPIRITUAL* JERUSALEM, AS JEROBOAM DID AGAINST PHYSICAL JERUSALEM ANCIENTLY.

Isaiah 22:20-22 is a related end-time prophecy. It begins, "And it shall come to pass *in that day*"—an expression that always means the end time, which is today. God says He will call a man and lay upon his shoulder "THE KEY OF THE HOUSE OF DAVID." This is not only about the key of David, but specifically about the key of the HOUSE of David—meaning the descendants of David, physically and spiritually.

God says we *must* have this message today, yet three nations of Israel are rejecting it and following the end-time Jeroboam.

## Flee to Judah!

When this nation can't bear our message anymore, the leaders will tell us to get out: "O thou seer, go, flee thee away into the land of Judah, and there eat bread, and prophesy there" (Amos 7:12). *Judah,* not *Israel,* is the biblical name of the Jewish state in the Middle East. The Philadelphia Church of God has had significant projects and activities over there, and these will apparently be well known. We now have an office in Jerusalem and a weekly worldwide radio program airing from there. We could have a stronger work there when this prophecy is fulfilled. People will know a lot about our work and our involvement in Judah. And when we are cast out, it appears they will force us to go to Jerusalem, or to a place of safety, which God promises not only in Revelation 3:10 but also in many other scriptures.

The "Israel" in Amos 7:11 includes the U.S. and the United Kingdom. Verse 12 brings Judah into the picture. Hosea 5:5 reveals that all three of these nations will fall together. Why is God so wrathful toward these three Israelite nations? Because they received the most blessings of all—they are the birthright nations and the scepter nation—yet are mired in unparalleled sin! In addition, all three of them rejected God's message. These three nations have a HISTORY with God. They also received the gigantic birthright and scepter blessings, yet they are totally ungrateful! Ingratitude is perhaps their greatest sin!

"Ephraim [Britain] shall be desolate in the day of rebuke: AMONG THE TRIBES [NATIONS] OF ISRAEL HAVE I MADE KNOWN THAT WHICH SHALL SURELY BE. The princes of Judah [the Jewish nation] were like them that remove the bound: therefore I WILL POUR OUT MY WRATH UPON THEM LIKE WATER. Ephraim is oppressed and broken in judgment, because he willingly walked after the commandment" (verses 9-11). What "commandment" is being discussed here? The commandment of Jeroboam anciently, who changed God's holy days, perverted the religious worship, and led the nation into idolatry!

However, this is a prophecy for the end time.

People in Britain, where the third of three prophesied overturns of David's throne occurred (Ezekiel 21:27), are going to be led astray by a modern-day Jeroboam. They are going to be led more deeply into sin. Now that the United Kingdom has decided to break away from Europe, it will be more desperate to trade with the U.S. This will entice them to follow Jeroboam's lead into disaster.

What a painful day it is in Israel when you look at what its people are doing. God has been so patient; He has given them so many warnings—but this is the LAST ONE! It all revolves around the time of Jeroboam.

## A Time of Extreme Urgency

Amos "warned the people that the supreme moment of their success was but the prelude to their doom" (*Soncino* commentary). This is what we are looking at with Donald Trump assuming the American presidency. Some people believe there was good news in his election. The Republican side was ecstatic. Right after the election, Rush Limbaugh said, "We just got our country back!" The "good news" is a mirage. It is a false hope.

THIS "SUPREME MOMENT OF THEIR SUCCESS" IS BUT THE PRELUDE TO AMERICA'S DOOM. A man is on the scene whose house God is going to take out by the sword! Conditions in America may improve for a short time. It may even help the Work of God. But its ultimate end is destruction. Our people are going to face THE WRATH OF GOD until they repent!

Amos 7:7-17 show that our time is very limited.

THIS IS ONE OF THE STRONGEST, MOST URGENT WARNINGS IN THE BIBLE!

"Then answered Amos, and said to Amaziah, I was no prophet, neither was I a prophet's son; but I was an herdman, and a gatherer of sycomore fruit" (verse 14). Amos had no formal seminary or college training. God simply gave him a job. Even without "credentials," God used this courageous man!

"Now therefore hear thou the word of the LORD: Thou sayest, Prophesy not against Israel, and drop not thy word against the house of Isaac. Therefore thus saith the LORD; Thy wife shall be an harlot in the city, and thy sons and thy daughters shall fall by the sword, and thy land shall be divided by line; and thou shalt die in a polluted land: and Israel shall surely go into captivity forth of his land" (verses 16-17). Amos had a very different view from Amaziah: He knew this was a message from God!

"Behold, the days come, saith the Lord GOD, that I will send a famine in the land, not a famine of bread, nor a thirst for water, but of hearing the words of the LORD" (Amos 8:11). How will this famine of the word come about? God's Church will be forced to leave. No one will be here to deliver the message anymore. When this faithful remnant of God's people is taken to a place of safety, God's message will cease, except what we do from that location. The nations of Israel have had over 80 years to heed this message, but soon they will not be able to even find it.

Verse 14 talks about people who are going to "fall, and never rise up again." This is talking about 50 percent of God's own Laodicean, or lukewarm, Church who will lose their eternal lives! What a tragedy—the greatest tragedy in this end time!

## The Lion Has Roared

"In that day will I raise up the tabernacle of David that is fallen, and close up the breaches thereof; and I will raise up his ruins, and I will build it as in the days of old" (Amos 9:11). God's Philadelphian remnant has worked to rebuild everything that God built through Herbert W. Armstrong. We won the copyright battle for Mr. Armstrong's writings and raised the ruins as in the days of old. God's revealed truth continues to be proclaimed to this world—for now. But all of this is God's doing; He gives the victory (verse 12).

God is using a small group of obedient people to fulfill this ruin-raising work!

Understanding where we are in prophecy—when God is giving His LAST WARNING to Israel in the time of the "Jeroboam end"—stirs us TO INCREASE our zeal for God's Work.

THE 2016 PRESIDENTIAL ELECTION WAS PROPHETIC. God puts His people right in the middle of it all—"in the midst of my people Israel" (Amos 7:8). His people have to be at the center telling the world what is happening and what it all means.

Look at the context for Amos 7. "The words of Amos, who was among the herdmen of Tekoa, which he saw concerning Israel .... And he said, THE LORD WILL ROAR FROM ZION, and utter his voice from Jerusalem ..." (Amos 1:1-2). Who is going to be the voice? Who will be the people who utter God's voice from spiritual Jerusalem? God has given us this message—we must proclaim it!

Verse 2 concludes, "and the habitations of the shepherds shall mourn, and the top of Carmel shall wither." The *Anchor Bible* says the subject here is A COSMIC HOLOCAUST—A NUCLEAR HOLOCAUST! GOD IS ABOUT TO SEND NUCLEAR FIRE! (see also verses 4, 7, 10, 12, 14; 2:2, 5).

We are all weak and sinners, but God promises to make us strong! WE WILL HAVE DIFFICULT TRIALS AHEAD. BUT GOD NEEDS PEOPLE WHO ARE EAGER TO DO BATTLE AND FIGHT FOR HIM, KNOWING THEY'RE GOING TO WIN! WITH THAT FAITH, NOBODY CAN PREVAIL OVER OUR MESSAGE.

"Will a lion roar in the forest, when he hath no prey? will a young lion cry out of his den, if he have taken nothing?" (Amos 3:4). God is roaring—and He wouldn't be doing that unless the destruction of Israel is *very close.*

"Shall a trumpet be blown in the city, and the people not be afraid? shall there be evil in a city, and the LORD hath not done it?" (verse 6). *Soncino* says, "Shall the horn be blown in a city and the people not TREMBLE?" If we are properly trembling at God's word, we will be overcoming and conquering our problems. God is building His character in us, but we first have to overcome our weaknesses.

"SURELY THE LORD GOD WILL DO NOTHING, BUT HE REVEALETH HIS SECRET UNTO HIS SERVANTS THE PROPHETS. The lion hath roared, who will not fear? the Lord GOD hath spoken, WHO CAN BUT PROPHESY?" (verses 7-8). We have to prophesy! We have so much wonderful truth and a powerful message from God that must be delivered to the end-time nations of Israel!

"Therefore thus saith the Lord GOD; An adversary there shall be even round about the land; and he shall bring down thy strength from thee, and thy palaces shall be spoiled. Thus saith the LORD; As the shepherd taketh out of the mouth of the lion two legs, or a piece of an ear; so shall the children of Israel be taken out that dwell in Samaria in the corner of a bed, and in Damascus in a couch" (verses 11-12). Again, this is a "thus saith the LORD" message. It is not from Amos or any man. IT'S A PICTURE OF A LION'S ATTACK ON SHEEP, BUT IT IS DISCUSSING ISRAEL—NOT SHEEP! God is going to tear these nations apart, until they repent. This is what it takes for them to get to know God and listen to Him!

This message has been saturating their lands, especially America and Britain, but they have refused to hear. God is going to bring them down, so they can finally get to know Him!

"That in the day that I shall visit the transgressions of Israel upon him I will also visit the altars of Bethel: and the horns of the altar shall be cut off, and fall to the ground" (verse 14). "Altars of Bethel" is talking about the Laodiceans (God's own lukewarm Church). Anciently, people could take refuge in the temple and grab the horns of the altar. By doing this, there was a good chance they would be saved from punishment because they were showing God that they deeply repented and wanted to change. Oftentimes, they would receive mercy from God. But in verse 14, God is saying that won't happen anymore! There won't be horns on the altar. They can't run and hide!

Those without God's protection who try to flee from one disaster will just be hit by another one! (Amos 5:19). But if we seek God and turn to Him, He will help us overcome, and we will LIVE! (verses 4-9). God will protect us physically and spiritually (Revelation 12:14). Even in a blistering message like Amos's, there is GOOD NEWS!

When we see this world race to its own destruction before our eyes, we know that a new world is almost here! Yes, there are difficult prophecies ahead, but they all lead DIRECTLY to the return of Christ!

"Behold, the days come, saith the LORD, that the plowman shall overtake the reaper, and the treader of grapes him that soweth seed; and the mountains shall drop sweet wine, and all the hills shall melt. And I will bring again the captivity of my people of Israel, and they shall build the waste cities, and inhabit them; and they shall plant vineyards, and drink the wine thereof; they shall also make gardens, and eat the fruit of them. And I will plant them upon their land, and THEY SHALL NO MORE BE PULLED UP OUT OF THEIR LAND WHICH I HAVE GIVEN THEM, saith the LORD thy God" (Amos 9:13-15). This is the wonderful conclusion Amos gives us.

There is a lot of bad news in the near future, but that is only temporary. All of it is good news because God is paving the way for Israel to know Him! Soon, everyone will be educated in God's ways, and blessed for their obedience!

TWO

# America's Real Enemy

WHEN HE BECAME PRESIDENT, BARACK OBAMA promised his supporters a *radical transformation* of the U.S. By the end of his first term, some supporters felt the change he promised wasn't coming fast enough. To them the president explained: "What's frustrated people is that I have not been able to force Congress to implement every aspect of what I said in 2008. Well, it turns out that our founders designed a system that *makes it more difficult to bring about change than I would like sometimes*" (emphasis mine throughout).

This is one of several statements the president made showing his distaste for America's Constitution. Mr. Obama is an outspoken critic of the Constitution and has long desired to cast off its restraints. In a 2001 public radio interview, then Senator Obama said the Constitution reflected the "fundamental flaw" of the United States. He characterized the supreme law of the land as "a charter of negative liberties. Says what the states can't do to you. Says what the federal government can't do to you, but doesn't say what the federal government or state government must do on your behalf."

THERE IS A REASON THE CONSTITUTION FOCUSES ON WHAT THE GOVERNMENT CAN'T DO TO YOU: IT AIMS TO RESTRAIN DESPOTISM AND TO PRESERVE FREEDOM! THAT IS ITS GREAT STRENGTH, NOT ITS FUNDAMENTAL FLAW!

America's Constitution has given more freedom to more people than any other government charter in history. It is a noble document that has inspired and enabled so many to attain accomplishments that any other system anywhere else in the world would have denied them.

You would think Americans would love the Constitution, but that is not the case in this country anymore. THE RADICAL LEFT WANTS TO DESTROY THE CONSTITUTION! The radically left Democrats are *very hostile* to the Constitution, and so are the mainstream media. Some in the media said Mr. Obama's only real problem was that HE DIDN'T ISSUE ENOUGH EXECUTIVE ACTIONS TO ENACT RADICAL POLICY. Many liberals now preach that for America to solve its many problems, it needs to ABANDON the Constitution. Most of the educational institutions would like to get rid of it. Many even argue that it is not even the supreme law of the land! Even one of the *Supreme Court justices* said the Constitution is outdated and should not be used.

This too is a liberal strategy to usurp power that America's founders never intended politicians to have.

An administration that ignores the Constitution when it doesn't serve its own agenda has *a lot* of power!

More recently, the attack on the Constitution has become even more vile. People have criticized it not only for making change more difficult, but also because it represents what they perceive to be *institutionalized racism* inherent within the American system!

"The goal of the Constitution was to make an agreement between factions known as states, which were built on the backs of black slaves." That's a paraphrase of what Alicia Garza said during a University of Missouri Black Lives Matter event in February 2016. GARZA IS ONE OF THE THREE FOUNDING MEMBERS OF BLACK LIVES MATTER, AN ORGANIZATION FOR WHICH MR. OBAMA AND THE RADICAL LEFT HAVE BEEN MAJOR SUPPORTERS. "THE PEOPLE VOWING TO PROTECT THE CONSTITUTION," GARZA SAID, "ARE VOWING TO PROTECT WHITE SUPREMACY AND GENOCIDE."

That is a satanic lie! How could Mr. Obama and the radical left support such a racist organization? The truth is that it was the system built by the Constitution that allowed the United States to become one of the first societies in history to completely *abolish* slavery!

Comments like these are a contemptible attack on the U.S. Constitution—*the supreme law of the land!* Such vile statements are stirring up a lot of anger and bitterness against the system of government established by America's framers.

THE CONSTITUTION IS BASED ON MANY BIBLICAL PRINCIPLES! The framers of the Constitution said it worked only if our people had a certain measure of faith in God and the Bible. Our people have forsaken God. And God is full of wrath because of it. He is cursing this land!

DO YOU REALIZE HOW DEADLY DANGEROUS THIS TREND OF LAWLESSNESS IS? Very few people do. But it gives insight into the real nature of the threat facing America.

THIS IS QUICKLY MOVING AMERICA TOWARD A RACE WAR AND RULE BY DICTATORSHIP OR TYRANNY.

## Lies

MR. OBAMA REPEATEDLY SAID HOW TRANSPARENT HIS ADMINISTRATION WOULD BE—YET VIRTUALLY EVERYTHING HE DID WAS IN THE DARK. MANY JOURNALISTS COMPLAINED THAT HIS WAS THE MOST OPAQUE ADMINISTRATION IN HISTORY.

That is the path to a violent dictator ruling America! And it wouldn't take but a few large and destructive riots to reach that nightmare.

In March of 2013, Director of National Intelligence James Clapper was called before Congress and asked, "Does the NSA collect any type of data at all on millions or hundreds of millions of Americans?" Clapper replied, "No, sir ... not wittingly." That was a lie, and he knew it.

Former Attorney General Eric Holder also lied to Congress—about the Fast and Furious scandal and about what his department did to reporter James Rosen.

As these scandals piled higher and higher, nobody could get administration officials to tell them *anything!* They LIED and LIED and LIED—and were *caught* in their lies! That administration covered itself in a *cloak of deceit*. In some cases, they even joked or bragged about their lies!

It is impossible to measure the damage that such deception wreaked on the fabric of our politics and our society. But *nobody seems to care.* When Secretary of State Hillary Clinton was investigated over the lies in the White House's response to the Benghazi attack, she responded, "WHAT DIFFERENCE AT THIS POINT DOES IT MAKE?" Apparently a lot of Americans agree with her.

That speaks volumes about our people. *We get the leaders we deserve.* Especially in a democratic republic, WE THE PEOPLE MUST ACCEPT THE BLAME FOR THE PROBLEMS!

MANY TRADITIONAL CHRISTIANS PRAY FOR MORE RIGHTEOUS LEADERS, BUT THEIR PRAYERS ARE NOT BEING ANSWERED. WHY? BECAUSE OF THEIR SINS.

What happens to a nation when people come to *expect* their leaders to lie? When people EMBRACE DECEIT? That is a far deadlier crisis than most people realize. Lies enslave and destroy us. Lies are the tools of tyrants. It is *truth* that sets us free. We should be passionate lovers of TRUTH.

WE MUST SEE REALITY: SOMETHING DEADLY DANGEROUS HAS SEIZED THE COUNTRY—FAR MORE THAN WHAT PEOPLE REALIZE. THERE IS A SPIRITUAL DIMENSION TO WHAT IS HAPPENING, AND YOU CANNOT UNDERSTAND THESE EVENTS UNLESS YOU RECOGNIZE THIS.

## Know Your Enemy

What is happening to America's leadership, its domestic policy and foreign policy is not just a quirk of history. The fact that Americans are casting the Constitution to the ground and encouraging lawlessness in their marriages, in their government and in their foreign policy has a very definite CAUSE.

We must *know our enemy* in order to understand what is going on in America.

Revelation 12:12 reveals that *Satan* is our deadly adversary. He is the one behind these dangerous developments. The devil is full of wrath, and he has gotten CONTROL of the radical left. The fruits prove it. These people want to bring this system down. They are deceived (verse 9). But the problem is much deeper than that.

Our people don't understand their Bibles as they once did. They don't understand the many scriptures about Satan the devil. He has his agenda against America, and it is prevailing because of America's sinful way of life.

Only God can protect us from this powerful evil spirit.

In his second epistle to the Church in Corinth, the Apostle Paul drew attention to this evil spirit being. In 2 Corinthians 4:4, he called him "the god of this world" who has "BLINDED THE MINDS OF THEM WHICH BELIEVE NOT." In 2Corinthians 11:3, he warned about how easy it is to be beguiled through his subtlety. In verses 14 and 15, he wrote that Satan actually transforms himself into an *angel of light,* and his ministers look like ministers of righteousness! This is an extremely deceptive being with a lot of power!

Paul cautioned the people to be careful and vigilant, "[l]est Satan should get an advantage of us: for we are not ignorant of his devices" (2 Corinthians 2:11). In any war, ignorance of the enemy is dangerous. We are far more vulnerable to the devil if we are ignorant of his devices, designs or schemes. The more you know, the better equipped you are to resist and fight! Satan is laying a trap, and you need to recognize it!

The devil's fingerprints are all over what is happening to America today. The rampant deceit bears the stamp of the father of liars (John 8:44). The contempt for law springs from Satan's own lawlessness.

Still, many people *scoff* about there even *being* a

devil—*while he is tearing them apart!* They know little or nothing about their Bibles. They don't understand anything about God, nor do they know the devil. Until they do, the problems will only intensify.

THOSE WHO FAIL TO SEE THE DEVIL BEHIND WHAT IS HAPPENING IN AMERICA TODAY WILL END UP BEING HIS VICTIMS.

Let me warn you *again* not to forget Revelation 12:7-12. Satan and MILLIONS of his demons have been cast down from a war in heaven. They are now *confined to this Earth.* Their time is short because of Christ's imminent return, and they are full of their worst wrath ever!

You see evidence of that wrath in this violent world full of treacherous deceit.

America is being attacked from within and without. There are failures everywhere: economically, culturally, politically, militarily and morally. Anyone who says there isn't a real problem here needs to open his eyes! We need to see what is happening to our nation.

THE RADICAL LEFT IS NOT OUR BIG PROBLEM. Ultimately, this isn't about a man or an administration; it's about an *evil spirit being* who is working to destroy this nation—and about why God is allowing it to happen!

God is *not* blessing America—He is cursing America!

## Time Is Short

God is *against* three nations in particular—America, Britain and the Jewish nation—because of their history with God, the birthright and scepter blessings today, and their unparalleled rebellion. NOT ONLY IS GOD NOT HELPING US, HE IS AGAINST US! (Ezekiel 5:8). (This is all explained in our free book *The United States and Britain in Prophecy.*)

Look at what God says about this through the Prophet Ezekiel: "Make a chain: for the land is full of bloody crimes, and the city is full of violence. Wherefore I WILL BRING THE WORST OF THE HEATHEN, and they shall possess their houses: I will also make the pomp of the strong to cease; and their holy places shall be defiled" (Ezekiel 7:23-24). This prophecy is about America in particular (for proof, request our free book *Ezekiel: The End-Time Prophet*).

"The king shall mourn, and the prince shall be clothed with desolation, and the hands of the people of the land shall be troubled: *I will do unto them after their way, and according to their deserts will I judge them;* and they shall know that I am the LORD" (verse 27). GOD BLAMES THE PEOPLE FOR THEIR SINS, NOT THE LEADERS! America is full of sins—and the *whole world* sees them! The leader may lead us to destruction, but God blames the PEOPLE.

God says He has broken the pride of our power (Leviticus 26:19). Many examples confirm that this is true today. Although America has tremendous power, we fear to use it. America has receded into the background and is declining rapidly.

Being weak *causes* violence and wars! The fact that America is withdrawing from the world stage will only allow evils to increase. As we get weaker, people will attack us more and more violently.

Why is America so *weak?* Study Leviticus 26. Again—it is BECAUSE OF OUR SINS. This is why God has brought this curse upon us.

The curses on America are plain to see. Prophecy *is* being fulfilled in events all over the globe! You would think that as times get worse and worse, people would look to the Bible to see what God has to say. Conditions are intensifying and getting so bad that *anybody* can recognize something is terribly wrong. *But virtually nobody is turning to God.* That is to our shame.

AMERICA'S PROBLEMS ARE A DIRECT RESULT OF AMERICA'S SINS. No politician is going to "make America great again," no matter what people think! I would like to see it happen, but it isn't going to happen in this age. *Everyone* will come to recognize that truth before much longer! God will make America great again *in the World Tomorrow.* He is going to solve our problems—in spite of our rebellion. He will SAVE America—*and the world*—at Jesus Christ's return, which will occur immediately after all these crises climax.

Notice the end of Ezekiel 7:27: All the punishment that is coming upon us is intended to *bring people back to God.* This is good news: In the end, PEOPLE ARE GOING TO KNOW GOD!

You absolutely need to understand the truth about what is happening to America today. We have been protected in this country for a couple hundred years. We have not experienced the turmoil that many other nations have. Yes, we were involved in two world wars, but God has given us a lot of peace. As a result, our people have settled into an *unreality* about what is really happening around us. They don't understand how deadly dangerous this world is!

This is not God's world. There is a lot of evil in this world. It is full of tigers waiting to tear people apart. It has always been that way. As Winston Churchill said, the history of man is the HISTORY OF WAR. Yet somehow we can't come to grips with that today.

Are you willing to face reality? Most people are not. A haze of deception enshrouds our world. It is absolutely stunning how easily the people in this land today are duped.

How could Americans allow the radical left to get such dangerous control of our country? Herbert W. Armstrong prophesied how and why this would happen over 50 years ago!

THREE

# The Origins of America's Dangerous Turn Left

MANY LEADING PERSONALITIES IN AMERICAN politics, media and academia have become dangerously radical. They promote policies that are weakening the nation economically, socially, morally, militarily and geopolitically.

How did the radical left gain such control of America? The problem is far deeper, and has been going on much longer, than most people realize.

During the Cold War, there was a lot of fear within

America about the spread of communism. Today, most Americans no longer consider it a threat of any concern.

But it *is* of grave concern. Few people realize it, but *many mainstream political views* in America today are identical to—and trace directly back to—the ideals and beliefs of communism or Marxism.

Bernie Sanders, who ran for the Democratic presidential nomination in 2016 and gained significant popular support, claims to be a socialist. The alignment between socialism and communism is significant. Many Communists even call themselves socialists. The fact that Mr. Sanders's views have so much support reveals how dangerously ignorant the American people are.

What do *you* know about communism? A growing number of Americans support the government taking over health care and other major segments of the national economy. They fail to understand the *dangers* that accompany a Communist system.

## Understanding Communism

Socialism and communism are alike in fundamental ways. Both say the centralized government—or "the public"—should own and control production, rather than individual business owners. Both call for centralized planning and control, which make for powerful governments that are highly susceptible to corruption. Socialism is considered the transition stage from capitalism to communism; in some cases, it is a less radical version that might eventually "mature" into communism.

In the early years of the Cold War, educator and theologian Herbert W. Armstrong wrote quite a lot about communism. We need to understand why he was so deeply concerned.

Mr. Armstrong wrote in the February 1962 issue of the *Plain Truth* newsmagazine: "[T]he 'Communist Party' is merely a trick term to pull the wool over our eyes and deceive us—a means of getting a fifth column into our midst—of getting the ENEMY'S GOVERNMENT into our very midst—leading us to accept it as a part of OUR government. Its only object is to DESTROY our government."

This is a basic truth. THE COMMUNIST MOVEMENT IN AMERICA HAS ONLY ONE OBJECT: TO DESTROY AMERICA'S GOVERNMENT! A number of nations have outlawed communism, yet America foolishly allows it as a political party.

Although the Communist Party USA currently has little power as an official political entity, the broader Communist movement has significant influence in many aspects of American politics and society. In an article about "the new communism," Alan Johnson, former professor of democratic theory and practice at Edge Hill University, wrote: "A worldview recently the source of immense suffering and misery, and responsible for more deaths than fascism and Nazism, is mounting a comeback; a new form of left-wing totalitarianism that enjoys intellectual celebrity but aspires to political power" (*World Affairs*, May-June 2012). That worldview is communism. And it is still bent on subverting and toppling the established order.

MODERN PROPONENTS OF COMMUNISM DOWNPLAY ITS SUBVERSIVE GOALS. BUT SUBVERSION IS ITS VERY FOUNDATION! *The Communist Manifesto* by Karl Marx and Friedrich Engels is considered the "sacred text" of communism. It stresses the need for a total overthrow of existing governments. The *Manifesto* concludes with some words that may sound eerily familiar to modern news watchers: "Let the ruling classes tremble at a Communist revolution. The proletarians have nothing to lose but their chains. They have a world to win."

The reason this may sound familiar is that students at the *University of Missouri* chanted a paraphrase of the line about chains in November 2015 as they protested, forced the resignation of the university president, and cried out for the whole system to be overthrown. Constitutional law attorney David French said these students are "REVOLUTIONARIES, AND THE REVOLUTION THEY SEEK IS NOTHING LESS THAN THE OVERTHROW OF OUR CONSTITUTIONAL REPUBLIC, BEGINNING WITH OUR UNIVERSITIES" (*National Review,* Nov. 9, 2015; emphasis mine throughout).

You do not have to look hard to find evidence of communism's influence in America today!

The New Left was a powerful political movement that swept through the nation in the 1960s and 1970s. Agitators and educators worked to bring about changes in homosexual rights, abortion, gender roles, drugs and other issues. The movement was closely tied to the "hippie" movement, and it achieved many of its lawless goals. The New Left was almost IDENTICAL to the Communist Party! The champions of the movement had stunning success in working their way into key positions in today's Democratic Party! Look at the radical left today. Is it any different from communism?

"With Henry Wallace's Progressive Party having collapsed, Hawaii's Reds changed their tactics. They went underground and concentrated instead on infiltrating the Democratic Party ...," Paul Kengor wrote in the October 2012 *American Spectator.* "For America's Reds, it was the start of a long march to operate within the Democratic Party, transforming it from the party of Harry Truman and John F. Kennedy to the party of Nancy Pelosi and Barack Obama." When Nancy Pelosi became speaker of the house in 2007, I was shocked. She had said the most obscene things I had ever heard a politician say. I expressed then that this was a disaster for the Democratic Party and for the nation.

Regarding the Communist goal to overthrow the government, Mr. Armstrong went on to write: "Of course, *if* it could do this peaceably at the polls, it would—but it knows it can't ..." (op cit). That was true at that time—but in recent years, these radicals *have* been able to win at the polls. This shows how much America has degenerated!

The radical left has gained control of the government and much of the country. What is the left's end goal? Mr. Armstrong continued, "[*I*]*f* it could do it peaceably at the polls, it would—but it knows it can't, so it does stand for the VIOLENT OVERTHROW of the United States government" (emphasis his). This is what it is all about. It has never been merely a political party—IT IS A MOVEMENT TO DESTROY THE GOVERNMENT OF AMERICA. And it has succeeded on an amazingly high level!

## A Foothold in Education

In the 1960s and '70s, America had many problems with rioting and violence on college campuses. Educators would ask who was in charge, and in almost every case, there was nobody in charge except the people who were rioting.

Soon, the New Left began to infiltrate these institutions and gain control. It was in the educational system that the left got its foothold into the nation: first in colleges, then high schools and even elementary schools. It is from the *educational system* that a nation gets its leadership. WHERE DID THE IDEAS OF AMERICA'S LEADERS TODAY COME FROM? FROM OUR EDUCATIONAL INSTITUTIONS.

Consider this: The Soviet Union pushed harder to establish communism than perhaps any government in history. Much of that push happened not within its own borders, but inside America! In 1970, KGB agent Yuri Bezmenov defected from the Soviet Union and escaped to Canada. He went to great lengths to warn Americans about the stealth attack the Soviets were waging against them.

Bezmenov said, "[O]nly about 15 percent of [the Soviet Union's] time, money and manpower is spent on espionage as such." The remaining 85 percent, he said, "is a slow process which we call either ideological subversion or 'active measures' ...." Most of this happened in American schools! Some of the main methods were infiltrating universities with radical leftists, establishing Communist-staffed newspapers, and holding international seminars with Soviet participation.

According to a former staff director of a Senate investigations subcommittee, in the years between 1935 and 1953, THE COMMUNIST PARTY USA "ENLISTED THE SUPPORT OF AT LEAST 3,500 PROFESSORS" (J. B. Matthews, *American Mercury,* May 1953).

Documents from the Soviet archives revealed that even after the collapse of the Soviet Union, the Communist Party USA received $2 million to $3 million each year from the Kremlin. This funding was to further the party's subversive activities.

Mr. Armstrong wrote in 1956 about the Communists "perverting our morals, sabotaging our educational system, wrecking our social structure, destroying our spiritual and religious life, weakening our industrial and economic power, demoralizing our armed forces, and finally, after such infiltration, overthrowing our government by force and violence! All this clearly disguised as a harmless political party! Communism is a worldwide psychological WARFARE!"

Communists first corrupt, pollute and agitate from within. But their final phase is a violent overthrow of the government. THEY AIM TO DESTROY THE SYSTEM, BECAUSE THEY CAN'T BUILD ANOTHER ONE UNTIL THAT HAPPENS.

The Communist attack from within America is far more significant than you may realize. We are staring it in the face today.

## The Real Watergate Scandal

In 1974, U.S. President Richard Nixon resigned from office over the Watergate scandal. It was discovered that the Nixon administration had broken into the Democratic National Committee headquarters and tried to cover it up. Many Americans these days know little about what happened at Watergate. To them, it is a scandal that brought down a corrupt president. But there is much more to the story.

President Nixon was a staunch opponent of communism, and the left hated him for it. At the time of Watergate, Rupert Murdoch, who owns Fox News, said: "The American press get the pleasure in successfully crucifying Nixon, but the last laugh could be on them. See how they like it when the Commies take over the West." He was only one of many people who thought that way.

What happened at that time has a lot to do with what we see today.

I remember hearing educator Dr. Herman Hoeh making this point in 1980. He said that President Nixon actually had come to recognize a conspiracy to work Communists into the New Left in America, and that he broke it up. "And for that," Hoeh said, "he was driven out of the presidency because a part of his plan involved preventing the far left from capturing the Democratic Party. And hence, Watergate. That's all a part of the story that most people don't realize. Watergate was not an attempt to see who was at some party of the Democratic headquarters; it was far more serious."

What happens if the far left gets control of the Democratic Party? Well, if it is elected, then it gets control of the government, the nation and everything that matters.

More evidence emerged recently backing up this view of what actually happened in the Watergate scandal. Geoff Shepard documented it in his book *The Real Watergate Scandal,* published in 2015.

Shepard served as deputy defense counsel for the Nixon administration during the Watergate hearings. "It was the first and, hopefully, the only presidential resignation in our nation's history," Shepard wrote in the *Washington Times.* "But it seared my soul, and I've spent many intervening years trying to understand how everything went so wrong" (Aug. 10, 2015).

"Four decades later, I've begun to appreciate what the real tragedy was. In one of the ultimate ironies of political history, it appears that the smoking-gun tape [an audio tape in which Nixon apparently sought to limit the FBI's investigation, and for which he was prosecuted for obstruction of justice] has been totally misunderstood, that the president need not have resigned, and that he was actually driven from office—and his senior aides imprisoned—through highly improper actions of judges and Watergate prosecutors" (ibid).

"John Dean, President Nixon's principal accuser, has recently acknowledged that the president and his defense team were totally mistaken about the tape and its significance," Shepard writes in his book. "If we had known the context in which that conversation had taken place, the president would not have had to resign, and in Dean's own words, 'could have lived to fight another day.'"

"Documents I've recently uncovered in the National Archives tell a tale of secret meetings, secret memos and secret collusion that will shock many Americans and that constitute flagrant violations of our Constitution and its Bill of Rights ...," Shepard wrote (*Washington Times*, op cit). THE PEOPLE WHO WERE SUPPOSED TO BE PROTECTING THE CONSTITUTION AND THE BILL OF RIGHTS WERE TRAMPLING ALL OVER IT BEHIND CLOSED DOORS. This was supposedly in pursuit of "justice" for a lawless president!

## Alger Hiss

"Shepard said the left's disdain for Nixon began when he was a congressman in the 1940s and brought down Soviet spy Alger Hiss, who was regarded as a leftist hero" (Townhall.com, Aug. 9, 2015). Why would a *Soviet spy* be a leftist hero?

Alger Hiss was educated at Harvard Law School. He clerked for Supreme Court Justice Oliver Wendell Holmes and was even in the delegation at the Yalta Conference where Franklin D. Roosevelt, Winston Churchill and Joseph Stalin divided up Europe. Through Hiss, the Communists were actually penetrating the

Truman administration; he was in high places in the State Department.

Apparently the left likes Soviet spies, because when Richard Nixon brought Hiss down, he made himself a target. Shepard told *Townhall*, "And what happened in Watergate, if you look at it in retrospect, the eastern liberal elites got control of the special prosecutor's office, and they had a power to prosecute. They criminalized prosecution. They staffed the place with all their friends" (ibid). He proves this in his book.

"Nixon came to national prominence as a result of this investigation," Shepard writes in his book, "and Hiss was convicted of perjury in 1950." They had reached the statute of limitations and couldn't really convict him of much, but they did convict him. "The liberal eastern establishment, particularly its many Harvard-educated members, never forgave Nixon for his leadership in bringing down one of their own."

SOVIET SPY ALGER HISS WAS "ONE OF THEIR OWN." HE CAME RIGHT OUT OF HARVARD, AMERICA'S TOP UNIVERSITY! These highly educated people had that spirit even then, and they wanted to get control of the government.

Most of these people HATE the Constitution, the supreme law of the land! They are LAWLESS! They can't stand to be constrained by the Constitution and law.

THE LAWBREAKING IN THE WATERGATE SCANDAL WAS *NOTHING* COMPARED TO THE LAWBREAKING THESE PEOPLE DID BEHIND THE SCENES. They violated the Constitution time after time because they have no respect for it. They have such towering respect for their *own intellect* that they think they know more than the Founding Fathers! This has led the U.S. into catastrophic problems.

We must keep in mind that they have a PLAN: Their

sole purpose is to DESTROY THE GOVERNMENT OF THE LAND. They seek to DESTROY THE WHOLE AMERICAN SYSTEM AND REPLACE IT WITH ANOTHER, which is really communism and tyranny. They want all of America looking to one man—like Russia looked to Stalin!

## Lawless Backroom Deals

"John Sirica is a disgrace to the federal judiciary," Shepard told *Townhall* (op cit). Sirica was the presiding judge over the Watergate trial. He colluded with prosecutors behind closed doors, and they worked everything out together. *Judges and lawyers are supposed to remain separate,* but Sirica worked with the prosecutors to bring Nixon down.

"Watergate prosecutors took the government files with them," Shepard explained. "These are government documents, and they should have *stayed* at National Archives and then subject to review with researchers like me. But three of the key prosecutors took their files" (ibid). Why did they take the files? Because they wanted to hide what they were doing. THEY DIDN'T WANT THE PUBLIC TO KNOW THAT THEY WERE UNJUSTLY DESTROYING A PRESIDENT AND TEARING DOWN A GOVERNMENT!

Though he had no real idea of the scope of these activities, Richard Nixon did see through a lot of what these people were doing. He had stopped them—and they hated him for that. They were determined to take him down.

"Nixon was done in by officers of the court," Shepard writes in his book, "the very people sworn to uphold the law and the Constitution—federal judges and federal prosecutors who met in secret and reached backroom deals on how best to take him down and secure conviction of his senior aides. THAT IS THE REAL WATERGATE SCANDAL ...."

Yet again we see *lawlessness* that is bringing America down! What will you have when the rule of law is destroyed? You will have nightmares like Stalin. What an example *he* set! Read some of Stalin's history. HE WAS A MADMAN WHO IMPRISONED, EXILED AND EXECUTED MILLIONS OF HIS OWN PEOPLE! He purged nearly all the top leadership of his army because he was so paranoid about people trying to destroy him.

## Not Just a Political Party

"Actually, the Communist Party is NOT a mere political party, in the sense Americans think of the term," Mr. Armstrong wrote. "IT IS A RUTHLESS, TOTALITARIAN DICTATORSHIP. It is run with absolute power by a few men at the top—all of whom are completely subservient to one man who is dictator-absolute! This one-man dictatorship is supposed to be necessary because there may be different *interpretations* of the Marxist philosophy. Therefore, to prevent division, they must have a supreme INTERPRETER" (*Plain Truth,* op cit). When you give one man that kind of authority and power, it will always bring about a tyranny!

"It is not *part of* ANY government. It IS a government—a WORLD government, which has set up, and therefore RULES the Soviet government in Russia. It is supreme *over* the Soviet government! Instead of being another political party as part of the party system of American government, it is a *foreign government* whose sole purpose is to destroy and overthrow the government of the United States and set up a foreign Communist government here instead ..." (ibid).

WE MUST SEE THAT THIS TREND WILL PLAY OUT UNTIL THE FINAL PHASE: THE VIOLENT OVERTHROW OF THE SYSTEM.

## Communist Mentors

There is an additional dimension to this crisis in America: an Antiochus type who was at the pinnacle of power, acting like something he is not.

Barack Obama was influenced as a youth by Frank Marshall Davis, a card-carrying Communist Party member. "Davis's unflagging support of Stalin's Soviet Union is apparent in a poem he wrote, lovingly titled 'To the Red Army,'" Paul Kengor wrote. The poem reads, "Smash on victory-eating Red warriors! Drive on, oh mighty people's juggernaut! ... Show the marveling multitudes, Americans, British, all your allied brothers, How strong you are, How great you are, How your young tree of new unity, Planted 25 years ago, Bears today the golden fruit of victory!" (op cit).

Anyone who publicly speaks of this crucial aspect of the former president's personal history is immediately branded a racist. But this is the truth!

In the mind of Frank Marshall Davis, the greatest threat to the world wasn't the Soviet menace, but "Anglo-American imperialist domination."

In his posthumously published memoir *Livin' the Blues,* Davis admitted to working with several radical left-wing groups in Chicago between 1935 and 1948. "I worked with all kinds of groups," he wrote. "I made no distinction between those labeled Communist, socialist or merely liberal. My sole criterion was this: 'Are you with me in my determination to wipe out white supremacy?'"

Davis harbored a deep hatred for Winston Churchill. "[T]he only people Churchill gives a rap about are the white people of the British Empire," Davis said, adding that the prime minister sought help from the U.S. to pummel "all other countries into submission." That is a monstrous lie! Churchill was probably the greatest world leader of the 20th century, and the fruits prove it. But after Mr. Obama took office, he got rid of the bust of Winston Churchill in the White House, on loan from Britain. This was a major insult to America's British allies. Apparently the president really believed Davis's teaching against Churchill.

It was Mr. Obama's maternal grandfather, Stanley Dunham, who introduced him to Davis, seeking in "Davis the father figure and role model that Obama lacked at home" (ibid). So he needed a father figure. He also had one in Jeremiah Wright.

Kengor wrote, "In 1995, an aspiring politician named Barack Obama published an autobiography called *Dreams From My Father.* There, Obama acknowledged the people who influenced him throughout his life. Among the most prominent influences was the figure that Obama gingerly acknowledged only as 'Frank'"—referring to Frank Marshall Davis, his mentor (TheBlaze, Oct. 3, 2012).

MR. OBAMA IS *NOT* THE PERSON MOST PEOPLE THINK HE IS. HE HAS A MANUFACTURED PERSONA THAT HE WANTS YOU TO SEE.

It is stunning how much and how often the government of this land is exposed for being deceitful. Everything revolves around *deceit.* Americans have practically come to accept this as a fact of politics today—but it is deeply disturbing and will have dangerous consequences!

Americans today are not living in the nation of our Founding Fathers, or even of our own fathers. *The ideological roots of the Obama administration were more radical than the public was led to believe, and it is certain that the devil used this fact to his advantage.*

The radical left and its Marxist ideas have gained control of the Democratic Party. Here is a quote from "How Black Lives Matter Is Bringing Back Traditional Marxism," by Thurston Powers: "It isn't surprising that Black Lives Matter [BLM] is a Communist organization—but the type of communism they subscribe to is. They are conservative Communists attempting to fold the progressive movement back into traditional Marxism. …

"The policy platform proposed by BLM in August did nothing to hide this traditionalism. Its calls for collective ownership of resources, banks and businesses, a highly progressive income tax, a guaranteed minimum income, and government jobs are lifted straight from the pages of Karl Marx's *Communist Manifesto*" (Federalist.com, Sept. 28, 2016).

During the presidential campaign, both Barack Obama and Hillary Clinton gave their full support to the Black Lives Matter organization. Mr. Obama and his administration even invited its leaders to the White House on several occasions.

The sad truth is that humanity will have to endure a time of intense suffering due to its own hardheadedness. But the wonderful truth is that this time of suffering immediately precedes the greatest event in history.

This world's systems of government and economics—not just communism but even democracy and capitalism—will never bring about good governance, prosperity and equality. However, at the Second Coming of Jesus Christ, this world will experience a form of government that *will* establish these things—a system that only He can implement!

FOUR

# The Deadly Deal With Cuba

In December of 2014, U.S. President Barack Obama surprised the world by announcing that America would restore diplomatic ties with Cuba after 53 years of hostility. The terms of the deal completely favored Cuba. Cuba did not have to abandon communism nor reform its dictatorial governance. The U.S. got *nothing* out of this deal.

What was this all about? We could write quite a bit about the president bypassing Congress and issuing yet another executive action to make this deal. We could say a lot about the dangers of America appeasing yet another regime that hates it. But the factor that is more significant than any of these issues is this: *The deal was largely the handiwork of the* VATICAN.

Pope Francis played a vital role in the president's decision. "Pope Francis issued a personal appeal to me, and to Cuba's president, Raúl Castro," President Obama said in his landmark announcement about it.

In early summer of 2014, the pope appealed to both leaders by letter, urging them to exchange prisoners and improve relations. The Vatican later hosted a clandestine meeting between the two sides in Rome. However, it was actually Francis's predecessor who put the plan into motion. In 2012, Pope Benedict XVI began pressuring the United States to normalize relations with Cuba. Francis carried on Benedict's efforts. After months of working behind the scenes, the momentous deal was sealed. Its announcement surprised the world.

So America has opened itself up to an unsavory regime just a short boat ride away. But this is about much, much more than that, especially when you understand the history of the Catholic Church and Cuba.

## Cuba and the Holy Roman Empire

The Catholic Church's history with Cuba dates back hundreds of years. In 1492, Christopher Columbus claimed the Caribbean islands, including Cuba, for Spain, the champion of Catholicism. Spain was ruled by Ferdinand II, the king who expelled or forcefully converted Jews and Muslims and who established the Spanish Inquisition—which is why you find almost no Protestants in Spain today! Just one year later, Pope Alexander VI commanded Spain to conquer, colonize and catholicize the "pagans" of Cuba and the rest of the New World.

Meanwhile, Europe's Habsburg dynasty was

becoming very powerful. Through marriage and inheritance, *the Habsburg Empire extended into Spain in 1516.* Soon, Spain was integrated into the empire. IN THE EARLY 1500S, CHARLES V GAINED POWER over the Netherlands, Spain and Germany. IN ROME IN 1530, THE POPE CROWNED HIM EMPEROR. HE HEADED THE FOURTH RESURRECTION OF THE HOLY ROMAN EMPIRE.

Charles continued to work closely with the popes, and the Roman church steered his empire. By the end of the 1500s, Spain had become the richest country in the world.

Much of its wealth and power came from Spain's conquest of the New World. Fleets of ships laden with billions of dollars in gold and silver crossed the Atlantic. And CUBA PLAYED A VITAL ROLE IN ITS WEALTH. Havana, Cuba, was the primary port for shipping all the treasure Spain was confiscating and mining in the New World. Ships ferried tens of thousands of tons of silver and gold from North and South America to Havana and from Havana to Seville, Spain. There, the Spanish spent it on the Habsburg's struggle against the Ottoman Empire and its war with the major European powers of the day. It also helped to finance the Catholic Church's inquisitions as that church tried to extinguish all other religions in Europe.

For many years, not a single European power was strong enough to stop the mighty and wealthy Holy Roman Empire and its ambition to colonize and catholicize the New World. This is part of Cuba's heritage.

Modern Cuba is a Communist nation, but it has only been Communist for about six decades—less than a lifetime. IT HAS BEEN A CATHOLIC COUNTRY FOR ALMOST 500 YEARS! Today, between 60 and 65 percent of Cubans say they are Catholic, so it's clear that the church's influence remains deeply entrenched.

Fidel Castro is now dead. And Raúl Castro is quite old. So the political equation could radically change soon.

If enormous changes occur, the Vatican could gain real power in Cuba.

## Cuba's Strategic Value

Many do not think the Caribbean is strategically important, but that's because the United States has dominated it for many decades. FOR THE CATHOLIC SPANISH EMPIRE, CUBA WAS THE SINGLE STRATEGIC PORT THAT SERVED TWO ENTIRE CONTINENTS. For Napoleon, Haiti served as the base of his empire in the New World. When he lost Haiti in a slave revolt, he gave up his ambition in the Western Hemisphere and sold off a massive chunk of territory in the Louisiana Purchase.

But there is a much more recent reminder of Cuba's strategic importance. If you are older, you probably remember late 1962, when the U.S. discovered that the Soviet Union was deploying missiles to Cuba. Sources told the Americans that some of the missiles were so big that the tractor trailers carrying them through Cuban towns had trouble making turns. THE SOVIETS WERE FORTIFYING CUBA WITH BALLISTIC MISSILES EQUIPPED TO CARRY NUCLEAR WARHEADS. AND THEY WERE ABOUT TO AIM THESE DEADLY MISSILES AT THE AMERICAN MAINLAND FROM POINT-BLANK RANGE.

Most authorities believe this was the closest the Cold War ever came to full-scale nuclear war.

The Soviets wanted to deploy and activate their missiles in Cuba without America finding out. With supersonic nuclear missiles only minutes away from

America's cities, THE SOVIETS COULD EVADE AMERICA'S MISSILE WARNING SYSTEM AND LAUNCH A SURPRISE ATTACK. I BELIEVE THERE IS AMPLE EVIDENCE THAT THE SOVIET LEADER NIKITA KHRUSHCHEV WOULD HAVE ATTEMPTED TO DESTROY AMERICA AT THAT TIME. What if Khrushchev had achieved his secret plan to *surprise* America? He would probably never have a better opportunity to conquer America—and he knew it!

Here is what Joe Garner writes in his book *We Interrupt This Broadcast:* "Addressing the nation in a televised speech, Kennedy told a stunned U.S. populace about the Soviet missile sites in Cuba and outlined his quarantine plan. Further, he warned the Soviets that the U.S. would consider 'any nuclear missile launched from Cuba against any nation in the Western Hemisphere as an attack by the Soviet Union on the United States, requiring a full retaliatory attack against the Soviet Union.' THE WORLD HELD ITS BREATH" (emphasis mine).

Would Russia have been so suicidal to risk a nuclear World War III, in the hands of Fidel Castro, if it had not planned an imminent attack on America? After all, Khrushchev did say that the Soviets would "bury" us. At the very least, the Soviet Union would have had the U.S. at nuclear gunpoint. America's foreign policy would have been neutralized.

However, something happened in Cuba. The Americans began hearing reports that missiles were coming in. But they needed confirmation. It would be difficult to fly over Cuba, a hostile nation, without getting shot down. But SOMEHOW, THE SOVIET PLAN GOT OUT OF PHASE. THE MISSILES ARRIVED AND WERE OUT IN THE OPEN BEFORE THE ANTIAIRCRAFT BATTERIES WERE FULLY OPERATIONAL. American spy planes spotted the missiles and brought home photographic proof of Cuba's nuclear buildup.

The Cuban Missile Crisis turned out to be a victory for America, a victory that could have easily been a crushing defeat. But it proved how strategic the Cuban islands are for anyone who wants to harm the U.S. With modern weapons, an enemy force could easily and quickly strike America's military and its cities.

## A Threat to America

If you were alive in 1963, you probably remember where you were the afternoon of November 22. That is the day you heard the news that U.S. President John F. Kennedy had been shot. President Kennedy was murdered as he traveled by motorcade in Dallas, Texas. Since that day, the truth about the assassination has been a mystery.

Lee Harvey Oswald, a former U.S. Marine, defected to the Soviet Union in 1959 and returned to the U.S. in 1962. Two days after the president's assassination, he was murdered by a nightclub owner under dubious circumstances. The Warren Commission, which investigated the slaying, concluded that Oswald acted alone. Most Americans still reject this explanation, and new evidence corroborates their suspicion.

On September 16, 2015, the *Washington Times* reported, "Three days after John F. Kennedy was shot and killed in Dallas, U.S. Intelligence officials told President Lyndon B. Johnson that they had confirmed that assassin Lee Harvey Oswald had recently traveled to Mexico City to visit both the Cuban and Soviet embassies, according to a half-century-old briefing memo, declassified on Wednesday."

THE AMERICAN PRESIDENT WAS MURDERED BY A MARXIST WHO WAS IN CONTACT WITH THE SOVIET UNION

AND CUBA JUST DAYS BEFOREHAND. It took the government 52 years to declassify this relevant information, and *still* large sections of the document are blotted out. "Oswald's travel plans were revealed in an unprecedented declassification and released by the CIA in thousands of Presidential Daily Briefings from the 1960s. Though the memos are decades old, about a fifth of their content was still redacted to protect sources and methods" (ibid).

For decades, the government's own official explanation was that Oswald was just a lone gunman. But the threat to America was—and is—much greater than that.

Did the Castro brothers have a big hand in assassinating the U.S. president? I'm not saying that happened, but with this report it certainly seems like you could make a strong case for it.

President Kennedy caught the Soviets as they tried to deploy nuclear-capable supersonic missiles to Cuba. The Soviets tried to put these missiles at point-blank range, less than 100 miles off the coast of the United States. ONCE THOSE WEAPONS WERE LAUNCHED, THEY PROBABLY WOULD HAVE EVADED DETECTION AND DETONATED IN MIAMI; WASHINGTON, D.C.; AND NEW YORK CITY WITHOUT ANY WARNING! THE LEADERS OF CUBA AND THE SOVIET UNION CLEARLY HAD DESIGNS ON DESTROYING AMERICA!

Do you suppose the Soviets and the Castros were wrathful against John F. Kennedy? His administration ruined a plan that would have either held America at nuclear gunpoint—or would have *destroyed* it in gigantic nuclear balls of fire! I would think that would make them very angry and revengeful! JUST OVER A YEAR LATER, KENNEDY WAS DEAD.

Yet the Obama administration opened the doors to diplomatic relations with Cuba. Now, if you want to make contact with the Communists, you can just go to Havana, 90 miles south of Florida.

Will this reengagement change the nature of the Cuban regime? Cuba remains a terrorist-sponsoring nation to this day. In those diplomatic negotiations, Cuba made *no* concessions. It got *everything* it wanted from its enemy, the U.S., and gave *nothing.*

Cuba has a recent history with Russia in designing a nuclear attack against America. COULDN'T CUBA JOIN WITH ANOTHER WORLD POWER TO COMPLETE THAT DESIGN?

You need to *beware* of what is happening in Cuba! This is a dangerous world. America is like a silly dove walking right into a deadly trap. Cuba isn't dead. Communism isn't dead. And CUBA IS REEMERGING AS A CLEAR AND PRESENT DANGER TO THE VERY EXISTENCE OF THE UNITED STATES! The assassination of President John F. Kennedy proves that foreign intervention in Cuba remains a clear and present danger.

## Who Does the U.S.-Cuba Thaw Benefit?

Where does the Vatican factor into all of this? One thing the recent U.S.-Cuba deal accomplished was to display to the world the kind of *power* Pope Francis has.

"Francis is a master of blending the spiritual with the political," said National Public Radio's Rome-based senior Europe correspondent, Sylvia Poggioli. "[He] has embraced the bully pulpit of the papacy, emerging as a daring, independent broker on the global stage" (Dec. 25, 2014).

What kind of deal is Francis brokering? Who does it benefit? The Vatican claims that the U.S.-Cuba deal is "in the interest of the citizens of both countries." Is that true?

First, consider whether it was good for the people of Cuba.

Critics of American foreign policy in general and of the U.S. embargo of Cuba tend to romanticize Cuba's ruling regime. That is a serious error! Under the Castros, the people of Cuba have suffered political terror and human rights abuses. Fidel and Raúl Castro have run the nation as a totalitarian police state, and Raúl continues to model it after the Soviet Union. Cubans are the only people in the Western Hemisphere who haven't been able to elect a leader in more than half a century.

When Russia and Venezuela, the main sponsors of the Castro regime, started suffering due to falling oil prices in the last few months before the deal, it looked as if the Castro government could finally collapse. That could have paved the way for democracy to finally prevail for Cubans. What the Castro brothers needed in order to survive was *an economic lifeline from their enemy, the United States.* And that is exactly what the pope and President Obama delivered. The deal also gave their criminal government international legitimacy.

Anyone familiar with the Castro regime's track record knows that legitimizing and propping it up is NOT in the interest of the people of Cuba! THE DEAL WAS BASED ON THE HOPES OF SOME AMERICAN LEADERS THAT THE CUBAN GOVERNMENT WOULD REFORM, BUT THEY REQUIRED NO CONCESSIONS. And it is extremely rare for dictators to voluntarily loosen their grip on power.

The normalization of relations, according to Rep. Ileana Ros-Lehtinen, a Florida Republican, "will embolden the Castro regime to continue its illicit activities, trample on fundamental freedoms, and disregard democratic principles."

This was a bad deal for the Cubans.

Was it good for the people of the United States? Under

the Castro regime, Cuba has acted as one of the Western Hemisphere's major sponsors of terrorism and drug trafficking. Legitimizing it is a victory for those who want to see America fall. Giving in to that Communist regime emboldens America's enemies.

As part of the deal, Cuba released Alan Gross, an American citizen wrongfully imprisoned for five years, and the U.S. released three Cuban spies. To U.S. enemies, this sent a clear message: A surefire way to win policy concessions from Washington, or to rescue your friends captured by the U.S., is to take American citizens hostage and hold them as long as necessary.

This placed America's weakness on display for the world to see. It also potentially endangered Americans by putting a price on their heads.

FOR AMERICA, THIS WAS A DISGRACEFUL SURRENDER. Mr. Obama undid a strategy that the nation had been using for 53 years, a strategy that might have been on the verge of toppling one of the world's most renowned criminal regimes.

Florida Republican Sen. Marco Rubio said, "[T]he policy changes announced by President Obama will have far-reaching consequences for the American people. ... There can be no doubt that the regime in Tehran is watching closely, and it will try to exploit President Obama's naivety as the Iranian leaders pursue concessions from the U.S. in their quest to establish themselves as a nuclear power."

Many American leaders like Rubio criticized the Cuban deal, but the pope was unfazed. Modern leaders would—and should—object to this kind of deal even more forcefully if they knew anything about the Holy Roman Empire. For many, the fact that the pope endorsed this deal made it *more* palatable! This shows that they really don't understand anything about that Vatican-guided empire. It looks so righteous, so *good.* But look at the history of the Catholic Church! Not only has it authored a lot of foreign-policy nightmares throughout the ages, but conservative estimates say it has presided over the deaths of more than 50 million people! Why do so many people just forget all that?

## The German Role

We shouldn't forget that the Vatican began to initiate this deal as early as March 2012, when the church was led by Pope Benedict. He is the German pope emeritus, and he has friends in high places in Germany. We need to watch this carefully, because BIBLE PROPHECY SHOWS CLEARLY THAT AMERICA, BRITAIN AND THE JEWISH NATION ARE IN GRAVE DANGER AND WILL BE DOUBLE-CROSSED BY A RECONSTITUTED GERMAN-LED HOLY ROMAN EMPIRE.

How will this happen? I think Cuba could be a significant part of the strategy. Nobody would suspect the pope of doing anything malicious or double-crossing America, but if you look at what the Bible says about the organization he leads, you will see that it is not what it appears to be. Study the history of every single time the Roman church started guiding European politics. You see a lot of blood spilled every time!

Look at the two men who were the main players of this deal: the pope and Mr. Obama. If you read our free books *The Holy Roman Empire in Prophecy* and *America Under Attack,* you know that these two men did not have the good of America in mind. Quite the opposite! If they work something out behind the scenes like this Cuba thaw, then you have to believe there may be something really big going on.

Pope Francis has made clear that he wants to topple the global system of free-market capitalism. "[S]ome people continue to defend trickle-down theories which assume that economic growth, encouraged by a free market, will inevitably succeed in bringing about greater justice and inclusiveness in the world," he wrote in *Joy of the Gospel* (*Evangelii Gaudium*), his November 2013 apostolic exhortation. "This opinion ... expresses a crude and naive trust in the goodness of those wielding economic power ...." History shows that our free market has provided far more *goodness* than the Vatican had when it was powerful! FRANCIS CALLED FREE-MARKET GLOBAL CAPITALISM "A NEW TYRANNY" AND CONDEMNED IT AS "A FINANCIAL SYSTEM WHICH RULES RATHER THAN SERVES."

WHICH NATION IS THE MODEL OF FREE-MARKET GLOBAL CAPITALISM? THE UNITED STATES OF AMERICA.

If Pope Francis is to be taken at his word, he could not possibly wish for the foremost capitalist nation to thrive, prosper and continue inflicting its "tyranny" on the world. If he is sincere in saying the capitalist system is a force of destruction, then he would feel not only justified, but *obligated* to use his influence to weaken it. And if decreasing U.S. power is among Francis's goals, he might have discovered that the Obama administration shared his thinking—to varying degrees on various policy points.

Bible prophecy discusses a massive double cross that the German-led European Union will commit against America. That double cross very well could include cyberattacks. They could knock out huge parts of our power grid and cause serious mayhem. Prophecy says those European nations are America's "lovers" right now, but that will not be the case for long!

Here is what Charles Krauthammer wrote January 1,

2015: "Vladimir Putin has repositioned Russia as America's leading geopolitical adversary and the Castros signed up for that coalition too. Cuba has reportedly agreed to reopen the Soviet-era Lourdes espionage facility, a massive listening post for intercepting communications" (*Washington Post*).

THAT "MASSIVE LISTENING POST," SO CLOSE TO THE U.S., COULD MAKE A CYBERWAR FAR MORE DANGEROUS!

When you consider what the Vatican is doing, you see how the Holy Roman Empire could also get control of that espionage facility.

Hackers routinely attack the U.S. government, military, infrastructure and economy. Most of these attacks are blocked, but hackers have scored some shocking successes. Industry experts warn that the nation is extremely vulnerable to such attacks.

Ezekiel 7:14 is an end-time prophecy indicating that future attacks will have devastating consequences! CAN YOU IMAGINE AMERICA, THE GREAT SUPERPOWER, BEING ATTACKED, AND NOT EVEN RESPONDING?

## A Coming Siege

Here is a critical point that most people overlook. George Friedman wrote in Stratfor's *Geopolitical Weekly:* "After the Soviet Union tried to deploy intermediate-range ballistic missiles there, a new layer was created in which Cuba was a potential threat to the American mainland, as well as to trade routes" (Dec. 23, 2014).

The Bible prophesies of a deadly economic *siege* that is going to strike America. It will cause one third of the terrifying damage that will be suffered in the Great Tribulation. THAT SIEGE IS ABOUT SOMEBODY CONTROLLING "TRADE ROUTES"—SO IT IS NOT DIFFICULT

TO SEE HOW CUBA COULD PLAY A STRATEGIC ROLE IN THAT.

The German-led European Union is the seventh and final resurrection of the Holy Roman Empire—that same Holy Roman Empire which, centuries ago, used Cuba so powerfully to fuel its wars. If the present resurrection were to move into Cuba again, it would be well positioned to carry out these kinds of attacks. The advantage is that it can do so within a cloak of secrecy, since Cuba is essentially a police state with tight controls on information. Think of the control that it could have. Think of how valuable Cuba has been to America's enemies in the past! You need to watch what is happening in Cuba.

Jeremiah 30 prophesies about God bringing the Great Tribulation on end-time Israel, which prophetically refers to modern-day America and Britain and its Commonwealth nations.

The Bible shows that this will all happen quickly. And we are getting so close to this time!

The seventh resurrection of the Holy Roman Empire is about to burst on the world scene. It will have similar ambitions to what Charles V and the fourth resurrection had, and all its other resurrections. And that includes the sixth one under the political rule of Adolf Hitler!

The seventh resurrection will cause many problems in this world. BUT IT ALSO USHERS IN THE BEST NEWS THIS WORLD HAS EVER HEARD!

The Holy Roman Empire will fight Jesus Christ when He returns. Christ will destroy that empire and usher in world peace, prosperity and joy forever. MANY Bible prophecies tell us of this wonderful event!

FIVE

# Where America's Race Riots Are Leading

On July 16, 2009, in Cambridge, Massachusetts, Henry Louis Gates Jr., a black university professor, had trouble entering his own home, and neighbors reported a possible breaking and entering. Sgt. James Crowley, a white police officer, ended up arresting him for disorderly conduct.

A week later, after conflicting reports of the incident came out, President Obama held a press conference where he said, "I don't know, not having been there and not seeing all the facts, what role race played in that. But I think it's fair to say, number one, any of us would be pretty angry; number two, that the Cambridge police acted stupidly in arresting somebody when there was already proof that they were in their own home. And number three, what I think we know separate and apart from this incident is that there is a long history in this country of African-Americans and Latinos being stopped by law enforcement disproportionately. That's just a fact."

Many law enforcement professionals were deeply disturbed by the president's remarks. Without facts, the president injected himself into this delicate situation, maligning the police with ugly statements and turning this into a very public race issue.

On February 26, 2012, a neighborhood watch volunteer in Sanford, Florida, killed a black 17-year-old, Trayvon Martin. Protests erupted across the nation. Accusations were thrown about of widespread racial profiling; the entire justice system was broadly criticized for its inherent racism. Once again the president inserted himself into a tense situation. "If I had a son, he would look like Trayvon," he said at a White House press conference. Later the president used the incident to talk about the difficulties of growing up as a black man in America, and how the police disproportionately target African-Americans. "Trayvon Martin could have been me 35 years ago," he said.

On August 9, 2014, a white police officer fatally shot 18-year-old Michael Brown in Ferguson, Missouri. Violent protests started immediately, before the case could be heard in court. Then they intensified after the policeman was acquitted. President Obama publicly criticized the police for coming down too hard on protesters: "There's also no excuse for police to use excessive force against peaceful protests or to throw protesters in jail for lawfully exercising their First Amendment rights," he said. He also accused police of "bullying or arresting journalists who are just trying to do their jobs." He ordered a review of the military hardware being shipped to state and local police.

In all three of these situations, the president was proved publicly to be on the wrong side. His false and provocative remarks increased people's mistrust of police. They further eroded an already dangerous loss of faith in the justice system. They increased tensions rather than settling them down.

Yet he did it again in April 2015. After Freddie Gray, a young black man, died in police custody in Baltimore, Maryland, protests against the police began before the cause of death was even known. These soon erupted in violent riots, in which downtown storefronts were smashed and police cars were damaged. Rioters cut hoses that firefighters were using to put out a fire at a CVS pharmacy. Looting and fire raged, and Baltimore burned. In comments condemning the violence, President Obama said that "some police ... aren't doing the right thing." He spoke of a decades-old, "slow-rolling crisis" that was responsible for much of the tension between law enforcement and the black community.

Race is a highly charged subject in the United States today; past wrongs and present inequalities create fertile ground for hurt, frustration and anger. This president used every opportunity to reinforce the black community's sense of grievance. Not just crime and punishment, but even issues like employment, college admissions, income and poverty rates are increasingly viewed through the lens of skin color.

It would be overstating it to say there is no racism among America's law enforcement officers. But there are some who are scrutinizing and magnifying this issue for evil purposes. They are using it dishonestly to justify or excuse some terrifyingly dangerous behavior. They are stirring up emotion and anger—but none of it is truly intended to solve the problem.

President Obama had said that he wanted to improve race relations in America. But again, we must look at fruits. What have been the results of his statements and actions? Practically everything his administration did when it intervened made the problems worse. IN THIS CASE, FAR WORSE!

A November 2014 NBC poll said that only 20 percent of Americans thought race relations had improved under Mr. Obama, while 38 percent said they had gotten worse. Among black Americans, it was even higher, with 43 percent saying race relations had gotten worse! An *Investor's Business Daily* poll found that ALMOST HALF of American adults felt that race relations had grown worse under Obama. And 1 in 4 said they had become "much worse."

Mr. Obama's efforts to "solve" race relations incited evils that are quickly becoming *far worse* than those they purported to solve! THE NATION'S POLICE ARE BEING UNDERMINED IN WAYS THAT WILL PROVE DEVASTATING TO OUR CITIES IN PARTICULAR. Accusations of police racism are heightening public mistrust of law enforcement and fueling a trend of violent race-related incidents and lawlessness. On one side, people in communities are developing a mistrustful, hostile, antagonistic attitude, yelling at police, assaulting and even killing officers in an increasing number of cases. Police are pulling back from doing their jobs for fear of attack. On the other side, the federal government is undermining local law enforcement and stripping it of power in an effort to centralize policing power at the federal level.

Anger among certain high-profile segments of the black population in particular is growing, and it is boiling over in rioting and violence with increasing frequency. Many people are framing the issue as a pursuit of justice. Some call it a revolution. Many are bracing for race war.

Many prominent leaders, both black and white, are deliberately fueling racial grievances for their own political gain. They use it to try to frighten blacks into voting booths. They have said violence like the Trayvon Martin case and the shooting in Ferguson are evidence of whites hating blacks. Rep. Charles Rangel, for example, said on October 30, 2014, that some Republicans "believe that slavery isn't over." The black congressman said, "[E]verything we believe in—they hate. They don't disagree—they hate! They think that if you didn't come from Europe 30 years ago, we shouldn't have immigration. Some of them believe that slavery isn't over, and that they won the Civil War!" If a Republican congressman made a similar statement about the radical left, especially African-Americans, he would be accused of hate-filled racism! These are abominable statements! Yet no one condemns them because that is the way so many of our radical-left politicians, academics and media personalities think!

These people are using *race* as a deadly weapon! The problems that will result are *far* more dangerous than they realize.

## 'Police Reluctant to Act'

I lived in St. Louis, Missouri, for 14 years before I went to college in the late 1960s. I drove through Ferguson many times. Even back then it was possible to see a growing problem involving race, lawlessness and a lack of respect for authority.

When Michael Brown was killed, Ferguson erupted in protests and racial unrest. The media inflamed the situation considerably. They essentially reported the event as a policeman brutally murdering an innocent boy out of racism—despite considerable evidence to the contrary. America has a judicial system to pursue justice in situations like this. Yet many in the media and the public, and even the government itself, act as judge and jury before the law has a chance to run its course.

Angry mobs looted and vandalized local businesses and demonstrated against police. Police officers came out in riot gear and with heavy equipment. That sparked further accusations of police racism, brutality and oppression. U.S. Attorney General Eric Holder criticized the police for being heavy-handed against demonstrators and criminals.

At the same time, business owners and workers were upset because officers *didn't do enough.* Many reports emerged of policemen simply sitting back and watching the looting, refusing to prevent or investigate it. When some people in a crowd began throwing rocks and other objects at the police, their captain told them to move back in an effort to ease the tension. No arrests were made. Former St. Louis County Police Chief Tim Fitch tweeted, "You did not see 'police restraint' overnight. You saw police reluctant to act."

People were looting, pillaging, rioting and

stealing—yet almost nothing was done about it. It is against the law to do all that, but WHAT CAN THE POLICE DO WHEN EVEN THE FEDERAL GOVERNMENT DOES NOT SUPPORT THEM? AND OFTEN EVEN WORKS AGAINST THEM!

Authorities in Ferguson reported that during the protests and riots, it was common to hear shouts of "Kill the police" from the crowds. During one protest in March, a man began shooting toward a line of about 25 police officers who were attempting to contain demonstrators. One officer was shot in the face and another in the shoulder.

Phillip Goff, director of the Center for Policing Equity at the University of California–Los Angeles, said police officers are now "generally concerned that the way the nation is talking about this is going to cost one or more of them their lives." Isn't that fear justified?

What we witnessed in Ferguson is more than a problem with race. It is a problem with LAW. What does it mean for the future of the United States when the police force cannot control the public?

Many Americans are uneasy about the violence. They realize that this could easily spread to other cities. Baltimore is only about 40 miles north of Washington, D.C., which could explode into serious riots at any time. The United States is filled with thousands of Fergusons waiting to boil over. These situations are occurring more and more frequently. Each time, the emotion is more heated. The violence is worse. The racial hatred is intensifying. At the same time, the media and the public trust law enforcement less and less.

The situation is filled with confusion. People are being whipped into a frenzy of hatred and violence. This is something the devil knows how to exploit. He is the god of this world (2 Corinthians 4:4), and he knows how to work on people's emotions.

Did you know that these burning cities are prophesied in your Bible?

ISAIAH 1:7 STATES THAT "YOUR CITIES ARE BURNED WITH FIRE." That is referring to OUR TIME TODAY—and you can prove it.

What took place in Ferguson is not going away. When you look objectively at the facts of these high-profile, racially charged riots, you can see why they are certain to grow much worse.

Few people realize how grave this trend is. You need to know where this is leading! In fact, the Bible prophesies that this type of racial tension is building toward a time of unparalleled suffering. Race-related violence in our cities is going to play a major role in the unraveling of our society!

That is the bitter truth that most of our people refuse to face.

## 'Stand Down!'

Many powerful politicians and people in the media believe that there is *justification* for the violence tearing up our cities. Many say they "understand" why lawlessness is overtaking these areas. Some even think there is something NOBLE about it—they see it as a kind of righteous search for long-denied JUSTICE.

THIS IS TERRIBLY MISGUIDED AND PERVERSE REASONING! It is multiplying the problem many times over!

In Baltimore, police were accused of *allowing protesters to commit crimes* without punishment. But *why* did they do so? In a press conference during the rioting, Baltimore Mayor Stephanie Rawlings-Blake admitted that she asked the Baltimore Police Department to "give those who wished to destroy SPACE TO DO THAT" (emphasis mine throughout). "We work very hard to keep that balance [between free speech and destructive elements], and to put ourselves in the best position to de-escalate," she said.

This mayor was trying to find a "BALANCE" between allowing these criminals "free speech" by DESTROYING THE CITY—and fulfilling her DUTY to PROTECT THE PEOPLE AND ENFORCE THE LAW!

She later denied telling the police to stand down. But police came forward and said they were in fact told not to stop the violence. For example, Michael Lewis, a Maryland sheriff who traveled to Baltimore to help stop the riots, said that Baltimore police thanked those who came from out of town, and said, "[W]e could have handled this, we were very capable of handling this, but we were told to stand down, repeatedly told to stand down. ... [T]hese guys told me they were essentially neutered from the start. ... I heard it myself over the Baltimore City police radio that I had tethered to my body-armor vest, I heard it repeatedly: 'Stand down, stand down, stand down! Back up, back up, retreat, retreat!' I couldn't believe those words."

THE EFFECT OF RESPONDING TO LAWLESSNESS BY HANDCUFFING LAW ENFORCEMENT IS GOING TO TEAR OUR SOCIETY APART! It is certain to add fuel to the fire that is burning parts of cities like Baltimore. Yet it is happening across the country: so-called leaders saying that law enforcement policies and procedures disproportionately affect racial minorities, and that the answer is to back down.

After the Baltimore riots, more and more police

officers became afraid to enforce the law. They know that if they get caught in the wrong situation, or they do something that might be perceived as racist, they could lose their jobs or face criminal prosecution.

The results shouldn't surprise any of us. In the year following the riots, Baltimore police arrested fewer than half the number of people they arrested the previous year. Police Commissioner Anthony Batts said his officers felt confused and "unsupported" after six officers were indicted following Freddie Gray's death. Arrest rates also declined because of interference from residents behaving in increasingly bold and aggressive ways against the police. "[W]hen officers pull up, they have 30 to 50 people surrounding them at any time," Batts said. Such interference makes it dangerous for a policeman to attempt arrests. These people are not just against white police, they're against black ones as well, because half of the policemen in Baltimore are black.

What happens when fearful police pull back? Criminals run amok! That is the effect when you undermine police authority, when you inflame bitterness, when you equate thuggery with a noble quest for justice!

In December 2014, two New York Police Department officers, Rafael Ramos and Wenjian Liu, were shot dead by a black man as they sat in their marked patrol car. The murders were apparently revenge for the deaths of Eric Garner and Michael Brown.

In July 2015, an Indianapolis police officer was fatally shot by an assailant with an AK-47-type assault rifle. Less than two weeks later, Lawrence Campbell killed a rookie New Jersey police officer by shooting him in the head. Other officers returned fire at Campbell, killing him. The Associated Press noted that the memorial that neighborhood residents built for Campbell, the killer, was larger than the one made for the murdered officer. Campbell's wife said her husband should have killed more police officers if they were going to "shoot him like a [expletive] dog."

Why is all this happening? Former New York Mayor Rudy Giuliani said he believed it is the result of "propaganda, starting with the president [Obama], that everybody should hate the police." Giuliani said black leaders, especially, have incited "strong anti-police hatred in certain communities."

Can anyone disagree? Those who insist that this hate-mongering and violence are somehow honorable need to look honestly at the *outcome* of such deadly reasoning!

## 'Far From Equal'

President Obama's wife was beating the same drum that he was. In May 2015, First Lady Michelle Obama used a commencement address at Tuskegee University, a historically black school, to speak about the trials of being black in America.

Her race affected the 2008 presidential campaign, she said: "[A]s potentially the first African-American first lady, I was also the focus of another set of questions and speculations, conversations sometimes rooted in fears and misperceptions of others." She and her husband, she said, "both felt the sting of those daily slights throughout our entire lives."

This was the first lady, who was in the White House because her husband won two presidential election victories by landslides.

What slights is she talking about? "[T]he folks who

cross the street in fear of their safety; the clerks who kept a close eye on us in all those department stores; the people at formal events who assumed we were the help—and those who have questioned our intelligence, our honesty, even our love of this country. And I know that these little indignities are obviously nothing compared to what folks across the country are dealing with every single day—those nagging worries about whether you're going to get stopped or pulled over for absolutely no reason ...." I tend to think that many times they *won't* get pulled over even if there *is* a reason, because policemen know what might happen.

Mrs. Obama continued, "The fear that your job application will be overlooked because of the way your name sounds; the agony of sending your kids to schools that may no longer be separate, but are far from equal ...." America hasn't even come *close* to equality, she says. She believes this country is filled with all kinds of white racism. (She didn't give one mention to black racism.) *We've come a long way, but there's a long way to go,* she says. *No explanation of how we've come a long way.*

She doesn't show even a scintilla of GRATITUDE. This couple has become *wealthy* in America. They have been given just about everything a country could give them. Why would she say things like that? What is she trying to accomplish with such statements?

She went on to speak of "the realization that no matter how far you rise in life, how hard you work to be a good person, a good parent or a good citizen, for some folks it will never be enough." THE CROWD BROKE INTO APPLAUSE AT THAT STATEMENT.

If you were sitting in that audience of mostly black people, and she said, *Even if we're nice and have good families and everything like that, it's never enough for some folks*, what are you going to do? How are you going to deal with that?

These kinds of comments feed a growing sense among African-Americans that this is an appalling problem that simply cannot be solved through normal means.

"[T]hose feelings are playing out in communities like Baltimore and Ferguson and so many others across this country," she said. AGAIN THE CROWD APPLAUDED. What is she saying here? These "feelings" are leading to *riots, looting, burning* and *attacks on the police*—and she is essentially excusing that behavior because of the way African-Americans have been treated!

WHAT ABOUT THE FACT THAT THIS NATION VOTED IN A BLACK PRESIDENT WHO INSTALLED BLACKS IN ALMOST ALL OF THE POWER POSITIONS? WHERE IS THE APPRECIATION AND THE GRATITUDE?

Stop and think for a moment. Policemen are being SHOT because of words like this! These are *dangerous* statements! Shooting deaths of policemen increased by *56 percent* in 2016 over the previous year.

What are we dealing with here? MORE AND MORE PEOPLE, ESPECIALLY IN THE BLACK COMMUNITY, ARE SPEAKING OF THE NEED FOR *REVOLUTION*—EVEN *RACE WAR*. COMMENTS LIKE THESE FROM MRS. OBAMA FEED INTO THAT MOVEMENT. HERS WAS NOT A SPEECH OF LOVE.

Some African-Americans don't buy into this drivel. You have to give them credit for that because they are taking a lot of heat for their position.

God loves every human being on Earth, and He has a wonderful plan to save every single person He possibly can. He expects us to love each other no matter what race.

But there is a devil, and he is a *liar* and a

*murderer*—and he is the god of this world! (John 8:44; 2 Corinthians 4:4). He rules! And whether people like to hear it or not, the radical left is leading people—including African-Americans—to their death! These leaders *think* they know where their actions are leading, but they are woefully wrong.

## Seeking the Truth

Consider this statement from President Obama at the time: "What I think the people of Baltimore want more than anything else is THE TRUTH." He is saying, *These are wonderful people. They may be tearing down and burning businesses, but I'm telling you, mainly what they want is the* TRUTH*!*

Is that true? The rioters themselves said, *If we don't get the verdict we're looking for, you're going to have a lot worse riots than you've had so far.*

When the president said they just want the truth, doesn't that mean there must be white people and policemen, both white and black, who won't give them the truth?

Statements like these from our leaders are all about DESTRUCTION!

I am not saying there isn't white racism. Of course they will find some. But do they ever find any black racism? Are those rioters really so good? We saw the Bloods and the Crips, rival gangs, unite in Baltimore—why? They directed the rioters away from places owned by black businesspeople so they would target the white ones! Yet that was OK according to the pathetic media, and the Democratic Party went along. These people just want the truth, after all. REALLY?

I DIDN'T HEAR ONE PERSON COMMENT ABOUT THE

PRESIDENT'S STATEMENT. BUT IT WAS SATANIC TO THE CORE! How many *mobs* have you seen that sought truth? That is just outrageously wrong.

Here is some truth: Most of the $800 billion of the president's economic stimulus money went back to the Democratic Party in indirect ways. Much went to unions, which would also come back to the Democratic Party. Almost $2 billion went to Baltimore. What good did it do?

Baltimore has a black mayor, a black police chief, a black district attorney, and more black policemen than white ones. The man they arrested, Freddie Gray, had used drugs for years, committed numerous crimes, and was caught running from the police, apparently with an illegal knife.

Here is some more truth: Ninety percent of the homicides in Baltimore are committed by blacks. Are the federal authorities really working to solve that problem? IF IT IS THE POLICEMEN'S FAULT, OR THE WHITE PEOPLE'S FAULT, THEN HOW COME 90 PERCENT OF THE MURDERS ARE MOSTLY BY BLACKS ON BLACKS?

How much value do *you* put on truth? This is not a time to be ruled by emotions. We need to be ruled by the truth of God.

## Taking Control Over Police

The federal government under Mr. Obama fueled people's mistrust of their local police forces, playing up the seriousness of these problems. One reason was that his administration was positioning itself to step in and solve them—while taking more power to itself.

On April 28, 2015, the Japanese prime minister was visiting the White House to forge an important bilateral trade deal. At a joint press conference during the question-and-answer session, President Obama chose to take the focus off trade and talk about the issue of policing. He said there were a handful of bad cops who need to be weeded out from police forces across the country. "Now, the challenge for us as the federal government is that we don't run these police forces," he said. "I can't federalize every police force in the country and force them to retrain."

It is odd that the president took the spotlight off the trade deal to talk about America's police forces—especially if, as he said, there are only a handful of bad cops. But it makes complete sense when you realize that his White House and Justice Department were pushing to do the very thing the president said he couldn't do: control local police forces.

White House insider and civil rights leader Al Sharpton expressed it best two days later when he told a crowd of reporters in Baltimore, "WE NEED THE JUSTICE DEPARTMENT TO STEP IN AND TAKE OVER POLICING IN THIS COUNTRY. IN THE 20TH CENTURY, THEY HAD TO FIGHT STATES' RIGHTS .... WE'RE GOING TO HAVE TO FIGHT STATES ...."

HE IS ADVOCATING A DIABOLICAL TYRANNY!

This isn't just sloganeering. If you pay attention, you can see how the subversion is being done. First, local police forces are being discredited. In a series of these high-profile race-related cases—Trayvon Martin, Ferguson and Baltimore, Eric Garner in New York—the Justice Department conducted its own investigation. The implication is clear: Local police forces cannot be trusted because they are racist. After these investigations, even if no wrongdoing was found, Justice Department investigators unearthed other data they said confirmed that police departments were racist against blacks and minorities—even departments with many black officers and in cities primarily run by black officials.

The Department of Justice, under President Obama, claimed the disproportionately higher number of crimes attributed to blacks relative to their population was evidence of police racism. It said this was due to "implicit" or "unconscious" bias by officers unaware of prejudices in their actions. They were supposedly subconsciously biased.

This was part of the Justice Department's justification for initiating investigations into police departments. It boasted in December 2014: "Over the last five fiscal years, our Civil Rights Division has opened more than 20 investigations into police departments across the country—more than twice as many as were opened in the previous five fiscal years."

The federal government was also making police departments in cash-strapped neighborhoods dependent on federal handouts. In December 2014, after Michael Brown's death in Ferguson, President Obama said he wanted to make sure police were using their surplus military and military-type equipment properly. He also proposed over $300 million in federal funding for local police forces to buy equipment like body cameras.

The implication was that if police departments want federal money, they must toe the official Justice Department line and adopt its policies. And they had to open themselves up to Justice Department advisers, whom many see simply as witch-hunters and agitators.

Here is some more *truth:* The president had federal staff moving into cities and taking over police departments in order to straighten them out! The federal government was grabbing more and more control. It had a *stranglehold* on the police. The Obama administration seemed to view each new prominent race-related police story that exploded into the news as an opportunity to seize more control.

THEY WERE TEARING DOWN THE POLICE, THE NATION'S LAST LINE OF DEFENSE! They undermined it to a great extent. DO YOU KNOW WHAT HAPPENS AFTER THAT? *Our cities will be burned with fire.* THAT NIGHTMARE IS ALREADY STARTING, AND IT COULD BREAK OUT AND SPREAD THROUGHOUT THE NATION OVERNIGHT! This is exactly what the Prophet Isaiah foretold would happen. In Isaiah, God tells us *why* these violent protests are burning our cities. He also tells us how to *solve* this problem—and His solution is TRUTH. Shouldn't we be interested in that?

## Prophesy Smooth Things

Isaiah addresses his message to "Israel" (e.g. Isaiah 1:3-4, and nearly 100 times throughout this prophetic book). Remember, "Israel" does *not* refer to the little nation in the Middle East. Actually, two nations in particular represent Israel in this end time: the United States and the United Kingdom. Don't believe me—you *need* to prove this truth to yourself. We will be happy to send you a free copy of Herbert W. Armstrong's book *The United States and Britain in Prophecy*, which contains ample proof of their biblical identity. God says—even *commands*—that we "prove all things" (1 Thessalonians 5:21). Jeremiah 17:5 says, "Cursed be the man that trusteth in man." So don't believe a *man*, but *do* believe God.

"Now go, write it before them in a table, and note it in a book, that it may be for *the time to come* for ever and ever" (Isaiah 30:8). The Hebrew expression for "the time to come" means the *latter day.* Isaiah wrote his message on a table, or a tablet, for the people of his day, but why did he write it in a book? Because this is dual prophecy. It is primarily for this *end time*, and God ensured it would be preserved for our day today.

Will you accept God's Word about this? Not many people will. Most tend to be like those described in verse 10: "Which say to the seers, See not; and to the prophets, Prophesy not unto us right things, speak unto us smooth things, prophesy deceits." People naturally don't want the truth, even though they may claim that they do. Most people want to hear *smooth things*, not truth right out of the Bible the way Isaiah teaches it.

They become more explicit in the next verse: "Get you out of the way, turn aside out of the path, CAUSE THE HOLY ONE OF ISRAEL TO CEASE FROM BEFORE US" (verse 11). THESE PEOPLE CAUSE GOD TO LEAVE! ISRAEL REFUSES TO LISTEN TO GOD; PEOPLE WON'T HEAR GOD'S WORD BECAUSE THEY'RE LISTENING TO SMOOTH THINGS. THEY SCOFF AT THE VERY WORD OF GOD ITSELF AND CAUSE HIM TO FADE FROM THE SCENE.

Pushing God aside is the worst sin of all! If you think there won't be repercussions, then you don't understand these prophecies.

Isaiah knew there was danger in delivering God's message anciently. It will never be received like it should be. Tradition says that Isaiah was actually *cut in half* because of the message he preached! That is how *violently* he was treated because he didn't speak *smooth things*. He loved those people and had the courage to tell them what God said and not the *deceit* they wanted to hear. As all human history has proved, that deceit always ends in violence, burning cities, chaos and anarchy!

What will all this violence do to America? What will

our ENEMIES do when they see this terrible division among the American population?

God says His Word is truth (John 17:17). But how many people really want the truth? Mr. Obama said the people of Baltimore wanted the truth. But did they really? Does ANYBODY really seek the truth? Very few do. Still, God tells us the truth about how to *prevent* suffering and chaotic violence that tears everything apart.

"Let them bring them forth, and shew us what shall happen: let them shew the former things, what they be, that we may consider them, and know the latter end of them; or declare us things for to come" (Isaiah 41:22). God specifically says we need to look at "former" events and "consider" them if we are to understand the "latter END" of His prophecies. In other words, to understand prophecy for this end time, we must also study history—specifically Bible history. As the Apostle Paul later wrote, the Old Testament was recorded for our learning today, "UPON WHOM THE ENDS OF THE WORLD ARE COME" (1 Corinthians 10:11).

Are *you* willing to hear what God has to say about burning cities, as well as the clear solution He provides for this crisis?

## God Has Spoken

"The vision of Isaiah the son of Amoz, which he saw concerning Judah and Jerusalem in the days of Uzziah, Jotham, Ahaz, and Hezekiah, kings of Judah. Hear, O heavens, and give ear, O earth: for *the LORD hath spoken,* I have nourished and brought up children [or sons], and they have rebelled against me" (Isaiah 1:1-2).

Most people would disagree, but God is speaking through Isaiah to us today! GOD HAS SPOKEN! "Hear,

O heavens, and give ear, O earth," He says. GOD IS ADDRESSING ALL THE INHABITANTS OF THE EARTH AND THE UNIVERSE! He has *spoken* to the righteous angels and to Satan and the demons. He has *spoken* to all mankind—all who have *ever* lived and we who are alive today. We *all* need to hear this message. He says, *Hear this! This is what will happen! You had better be careful, or you will have disastrous trouble!*

About 25 percent of the New Testament is comprised of quotes from the Old Testament, and *most* of those quotes come from the book of Isaiah, so this is a New Testament message as well. This is telling us what is happening *today.*

If people want to impugn the Bible and scoff at it, they can do that—but God says the burning of cities will intensify if we don't learn what He is telling us. The time is coming soon when the scoffers are going to vanish like snow under the hot sun because everything will have come to pass *exactly* as God has *spoken* it to us!

"The ox knoweth his owner, and the ass his master's crib: but Israel doth not know, my people doth not consider" (verse 3). What does Israel not know? Its people DON'T KNOW GOD, and they don't know the Bible because they won't listen to God and to His messengers, and they have *caused* Him to go away from them.

"Ah sinful nation, a people laden with iniquity, a seed of evildoers, children that are corrupters: they have FORSAKEN THE LORD, they have provoked the Holy One of Israel unto anger, they are gone away backward. Why should ye be stricken any more? …" (verses 4-5). GOD IS PLEADING WITH US: *WHY SHOULD YOU BE STRICKEN ANY MORE? WHY NOT LISTEN TO ME AND SOLVE THESE CRISES?*

Will you listen to God so YOU don't have to suffer?

## Sick Head, Faint Heart

Isaiah 1:5 concludes by saying, "[Y]e will revolt more and more: THE WHOLE HEAD IS SICK, AND THE WHOLE HEART FAINT."

The "head" refers to the leaders of modern Israel. God says "the *whole head* is SICK"! The minds of our leaders are SICK with deceitful human reasoning that is anti-God! Their decisions are perverse and leading to greater and greater calamities!

Authorities in Baltimore decided to give protesters "space" to commit lawless acts. Then they hastily indicted six police officers who had been involved in Freddie Gray's death, charging them with murder and manslaughter. These charges were all later disproved in court—according to the justice system, these officers committed no crimes. Why did they initially lay down such harsh charges? TO TRY TO PACIFY THE CROWD. The angry mob was howling for the blood of these policemen. The Baltimore state attorney essentially gave them the indictments they were looking for and expected them to calm down.

That decision was almost certainly made out of *fear* of the rioters—if it wasn't a racially motivated effort to "seek justice" at the expense of the law. State and federal authorities tried to show themselves *sympathetic* to the criminals—even more than to the innocent people of Baltimore!

Whatever their reasons for doing so, the big lesson this sent to protesters and agitators across the country was clear: *Lawlessness gets results. Violent protests are a legitimate, effective means of seeking justice.* What a dangerous example and precedent! Already you can see how each time a high-profile case like this hits the news, public anger boils to the surface faster and more aggressively than the time before. There is a rising sense among a growing portion of the population that the inequalities and injustices in society *must* be met with violence!

At the same time, decisions like the one to have police "stand down," or to make an example of these six policemen, DESTROY the morale of the nation's law enforcers. Certainly there is no excuse for police brutality. But how many *good* policemen will fear to do their jobs—jobs that are sure to become even more dangerous as disorder intensifies—knowing the state might side with the criminals, or knowing they could be unjustly prosecuted? The institution that protects and preserves the stability of America's cities is being undermined and weakened.

AS THE VIOLENCE SPREADS, THE WILL TO STOP IT SHRINKS. "THE WHOLE HEAD IS SICK, AND THE WHOLE HEART FAINT," God says. In the face of such problems, our people have become *fainthearted*—too *cowardly* to do what needs to be done. We are afraid of almost *everything*, it seems, because we don't know God and don't let Him empower us and give us the courage we need.

## Burning Cities

Look now at this lightning-bolt prophecy explaining the terrible CONSEQUENCES of our grave national sins: "Your country is desolate, YOUR CITIES ARE BURNED WITH FIRE: your land, strangers devour it in your presence, and it is desolate, as overthrown by strangers" (Isaiah 1:7).

THIS PROPHECY IS A GUARANTEE THAT OUR NATIONAL PROBLEMS ARE GOING TO GET WORSE BECAUSE WE WON'T LISTEN TO GOD! He is *pleading* with us to hear His message, to *listen* to Him, and to *fear* Him. But we refuse, and the degeneration rapidly grows worse!

Between 2010 and 2015, about $1.8 billion of stimulus money was spent on Baltimore for education, teachers' unions, and employment and social benefits. Did that solve Baltimore's problems? No—the crises grew WORSE. Money is not the solution, and it never has been. The problems go much deeper than that.

GOD IS TRYING TO HELP US SEE THAT SOMETHING IS FRIGHTFULLY WRONG! He says, *DON'T POINT FINGERS AT THE LEADERS, BECAUSE YOU'RE ALL TO BLAME!*

This is not a smooth message, but it is the *truth.* God blames us all! We are trying to solve these problems our way, and it simply cannot be done.

Anciently Israel was known as "Zion" (e.g. Psalm 9:11; 132:13). Isaiah 1:8 refers to "the daughter of Zion." That is another indication that this is a *prophecy*—not for Israel in Isaiah's time but for the modern *descendants* of Israel.

Spiritually, Zion applies to God's own Church.

Verse 8 prophesies that "the daughter of Zion" will be "left as a cottage in a vineyard, as a lodge in a garden of cucumbers, as a besieged city." This is a poetic description of modern Israel's destruction: Our nations will be like a little hut after all the harvest is over—abandoned and desolate. That is true of the Work of God in His rebellious Church, and also of America, the great superpower of Israel. They have no impact as they should because they have departed from God and sought after smooth things and deceits that are anti-God.

"Except the LORD of hosts had left unto us a very small remnant, we should have been as Sodom, and we should have been like unto Gomorrah" (verse 9). Spiritually, God leaves a very small remnant that does what He says and tells it like it is.

"Hear the word of the LORD, ye rulers of Sodom; give ear unto the law of our God, ye people of Gomorrah" (verse 10). HEAR WHAT GOD HAS TO SAY! Do you hear it? God says conditions will get so bad that you *are* going to hear, but for most people it will be too late physically. We need to hear the truth of God as never before, because conditions are worsening. We need to hear what God speaks—and He *does* speak to us if we will hear!

Here is what happens because of our sins: "And when ye spread forth your hands, I will hide mine eyes from you: yea, WHEN YE MAKE MANY PRAYERS, I WILL NOT HEAR: your hands are full of blood" (verse 15). God is addressing His own rebellious Church that isn't delivering His message—the hands of those people are full of blood because of their failure. God holds them responsible for the bloodshed.

GOD IS ALSO TALKING TO THE PEOPLE IN THE NATIONS OF ISRAEL WHO ARE PRAYING TO HIM FOR HELP AND ANSWERS. He says, *IF YOU'RE NOT HEARING MY MESSAGE, I WILL NOT HEAR YOUR PRAYERS. EVEN IF YOU PRAY MANY PRAYERS AND LOOK SO RIGHTEOUS, IF YOU DON'T DO WHAT I TELL YOU, I WILL NOT HEAR YOU.*

This is an "unsmooth" truth! This is a super-critical verse because it shows why the nations of Israel do not have God's power. There was a time when this prophecy would strike fear in our minds, but not anymore. Most people respond with a scoffing attitude.

The number one need we have is God's power, yet God says it is sadly lacking in our nations and most of His Church members. But God gives POWER to His very elect to do great things, to do heroic *exploits* (Daniel 11:32).

The Apostle Paul said, "I can do ALL things through Christ which strengtheneth me" (Philippians 4:13). Paul was a powerful man because God EMPOWERED him through His Spirit. That is the way it *should* be for our people today.

## 'Come and Reason With Me'

"Come now, and let us reason together, saith the LORD: though your sins be as scarlet, they shall be as white as snow ..." (Isaiah 1:18). God says that if we will just listen to Him and *hear* what He has to say, our sins will become like white wool.

This verse correctly reads: "Come and reason with me." How do you do that? You reason with God in His Bible. He says He will reveal truth to you through His little remnant. God's faithful people have His truth and speak it, because they are empowered by Him. And He reveals more and more to them, as long as they heed His warning.

"If ye be willing and obedient, ye shall eat the good of the land: But if ye refuse and rebel, YE SHALL BE DEVOURED WITH THE SWORD: for the mouth of the LORD hath spoken it" (verses 19-20). The rioters and violent protesters may think they will come out of this as the victors, but God says no. *Your enemies from without are going to exploit the division, violence and anarchy within your nation! There won't be* ANY *winners from within the nation!* That is what God is saying.

Bible prophecies make clear that even worse and more violent protests and riots are going to erupt in American (and British) cities. This will fatally weaken the nation and lead to curses of a far GREATER MAGNITUDE!

We must heed what God says in the book of Isaiah!

GOD WARNS THAT WE ARE GOING TO HAVE TO SUFFER UNTIL WE GET THIS MESSAGE! There is no other way!

But you also must see the bigger picture. Those individuals who do respond and heed God's warning, He will protect. He doesn't want people to suffer through these curses. And we must ALL see that these burning cities are prophesied to occur in the *very last days* of America's existence as a strong world power—which is actually RIGHT BEFORE THE MESSIAH RETURNS TO RULE THIS EARTH!

YES, AMERICA'S BURNING CITIES PRESAGE THE SECOND COMING OF JESUS CHRIST TO THIS EARTH! THIS IS ALL A SIGN THAT HIS RETURN IS IMMINENT!

When He returns, He will *end* all racism and injustice permanently. He will rule this world with a rod of iron and with His love!

SIX

# The Most Dangerous Lie in History

IN 2015, THE U.S. SPEARHEADED AN INTERNATIONAL effort to negotiate a nuclear deal with Iran. When the agreement was concluded, many people were elated, but there should have been no celebration. What is at stake is nothing less than HUMAN SURVIVAL. The world needed something that would have pulled us *away* from the brink of annihilation, but this deal did just the opposite.

If you doubt that it is about human survival, just talk to the Jewish nation Iran repeatedly says it wants to wipe off the map. Israel believes its *survival* rests on whether or not Iran gets a nuclear bomb!

Even during the nuclear talks, Iranian groups repeatedly chanted "Death to Israel" and "Death to America." Iran's leaders continued to call Israel "the little Satan" and America "the great Satan." They have a history of hating America and wanting to wipe our influence off the Earth.

The whole nuclear agreement hinges on trust. Can Iran be trusted? This nation has broken its agreements with the United Nations over nuclear inspections around 20 times. The inspections never achieved anything. Iran just kept deceiving the UN, buying time to continue its nuclear activities—and the UN and the rest of the world played along. Do you think its behavior will change because of *this* agreement?

Since the Iranian Revolution, the majority of Americans have rightfully held an unfavorable view of Iran. Most politically aware Americans were well aware of the anti-American and anti-Semitic ranting of Iran's mullahs. Many worried about the Islamic Republic's development of nuclear weapons and how the mullahs would use them. So how did President Obama get the deal to go through? His methods reveal so much about his administration, and about him personally!

For many months before the deal was made, a key member of Obama's inner circle was working hard to lay people's fears to rest. At a meeting with Democratic Party activists in 2014, Benjamin Rhodes, then deputy national security adviser for strategic communication, argued that a nuclear agreement with Tehran was "the best opportunity we've had to resolve the Iranian [nuclear] issue." He said this deal was "probably the biggest thing President Obama will do in his second term on foreign policy."

UNAWARE THAT THE MEETING WAS RECORDED, RHODES

CONFIDED TO HIS GUESTS THAT PRESIDENT OBAMA WAS PLANNING TO SIDELINE CONGRESS: "We're already kind of thinking through, how do we structure a deal so we don't necessarily require legislative action right away," he said.

After the deal was implemented on January 16, 2016, Rhodes explained in a *New York Times Magazine* interview that if he wanted to get anyone other than those on the hard left to accept a deal with Tehran, HE HAD TO LIE. He blatantly and willfully deceived what he considered a corrupt and inexperienced American media about all sorts of things. "THE AVERAGE REPORTER WE TALK TO IS 27 YEARS OLD," Rhodes explained, "AND THEIR ONLY REPORTING EXPERIENCE CONSISTS OF BEING AROUND POLITICAL CAMPAIGNS. ... THEY LITERALLY KNOW NOTHING."

Rhodes admitted to fashioning a story about how the administration's negotiations began. He told the press that a "thaw" in American-Iranian relations was made possible by the election of President Hassan Rouhani and other Iranian "moderates" in the summer of 2013. Yet he bluntly admitted that he wasn't actually sure whether Rouhani was a "moderate" or not. Then he bragged about how easy it was to deceive journalists in order to get this deal passed without congressional approval.

What a spectacle America has become to the world! It is as if lawless *children* are in charge of America's foreign policy!

Just days before the deal was signed, Iran's president marched with a huge crowd of Iranians who were holding "Death to Israel" and "Death to America" signs. That reaction alone should be enough to trumpet the fact that the Western world—especially America—was humiliated through this deal. Here is another case where we must judge not by *words,* but BY FRUITS. Iran's fruits show it will violate this agreement. But this time, the stakes are much higher!

Here is what Charles Krauthammer said about the nuclear deal: "I think the real issue here is not the fact that we did ransom, because I think people know that we do it in a lot of disguised ways. ... IT'S THAT THEY LIED AND THEY LIE SHAMELESSLY AND THEY LIE WHEN THE LIE IS UNCOVERED. THAT'S WHAT IS SO SCARY, AND THEY LIE ABOUT THE ENTIRE IRAN DEAL. This is the tip of the iceberg. ... Every item on the Iran deal that we were promised, we would hold the line on X, Y and Z, we did this or we are getting inspections ... THEY LIED ALL THE WAY THROUGH and that deal is shot through with denials, with all kinds of statements that are not so, and WE ARE GOING TO SUFFER. THAT'S GOING TO BE A LOT WORSE THAN ANYTHING THAT COMES OUT OF THIS RANSOM PAYMENT" (Aug. 18, 2016; emphasis mine throughout).

## The Cause of America's Curses

The Bible has a lot to say about the state of America today. It explains the inspiring reason *why* this nation was so great, and why it has been so richly blessed.

THE BIBLE ALSO *PROPHESIES* THAT THESE BLESSINGS WILL BE *REMOVED* IN OUR DAY—REPLACED BY TERRIBLE CURSES—BECAUSE OF *THE SINS OF THE PEOPLE.* Yes, as a consequence of deep and multiplying materialism, selfishness, lust, immorality and idolatry among the American people, those prophesied curses are descending rapidly!

America's problems are *spiritual*—and solving them requires spiritual solutions, starting with repentance! But Americans are too entrenched in their sin to do that. So the national curses are going to get far worse before the situation ever gets better.

When you understand this spiritual dimension, it becomes far easier to understand why President Obama did the things he did, and why the damage he caused will not be reversed by putting a different man into his office.

The damage President Obama wreaked is beyond repair by human beings! I hope what you have read in *Great Again* has helped you to see how his decisions and policies fulfilled significant Bible prophecies about America's destruction!

But the Bible also explains God's ultimate *purpose* for allowing these curses to descend on the U.S. Whenever God punishes, He does so to turn people back to Himself. Scripture prophesies that the curses America is experiencing today *are* actually a prelude to national revitalization and restoration!

America *will,* in fact, one day soon become GREAT AGAIN!

## Nuclear Warfare Prophesied!

The Obama administration's handling of Syria and Iran was a monumental disaster. And I see little to show that the situation will change substantially under President Trump. The nation's enemies shake their fists at us at every turn, and we let them get away with it. America's credibility is in tatters.

In Leviticus 26:19, God warned that if our peoples descended into abject sin, He would *break the pride of our power.* And so He has! We have seen a complete collapse of will and power in America. What a terrible end to a superpower!

We live in exceedingly dangerous times. *We are talking about nuclear bombs!* That makes America's weakness all the more alarming and disgraceful.

Many people—including high-profile academics and intellectuals in the U.S.—*cheer* the thought of America's power coming to an end. But the same biblical prophecies that foretold America's fall *also* reveal the nightmares that will unfold once other world powers take control.

In the 1930s and 1940s, Hitler and the Nazis kept pushing and pushing, yet Britain and America just hoped the problem would go away. They thought Hitler could be appeased with words and treaties. But that did not stop him. Only superior will and power stops a tyrant or madman.

NO WORDS WILL STOP THIS KING OF TERROR. THE IRANIAN LEADER BELIEVES THAT CAUSING A NUCLEAR CATACLYSM WILL HASTEN THE COMING OF HIS MESSIAH. NO MATTER WHAT HAPPENS, THESE RELIGIOUS ZEALOTS BELIEVE THEY ARE WINNERS.

NO OTHER NUCLEAR POWER THINKS LIKE THAT! IT MAKES NUCLEAR WAR INEVITABLE!

Mr. Obama's appeasement of and support for the Iranian regime cannot be explained logically. Such a catastrophic policy can only be understood in the context of the *satanic deception* that blankets this *entire world* (Revelation 12:9). Those efforts shoved the world closer to the brink of nuclear annihilation—and nothing could please the devil more! "[T]hat old serpent, called the Devil, and Satan, which deceiveth the whole world" had his fingerprints all over those developments. He passionately hates mankind and loves causing the death of millions—even billions!

This explosive situation will result in nuclear war. Jesus Christ prophesied the outcome of these problems in Matthew 24:21-22. He said the coming "great tribulation" would be *worse* than any in mankind's long, tragic history! He warned that unless these perilous days were *shortened,* NO FLESH WOULD BE SAVED ALIVE! Passages like this and Daniel 12:1 describe a time of such catastrophic destruction that they could only apply to weapons of mass destruction. Isaiah 6:11, Jeremiah 2:15 and many other prophecies foretell cities without even one inhabitant. Only nuclear weapons could cause that.

NUCLEAR WARFARE IS NEAR! IT IS PROPHESIED OVER 100 TIMES IN BIBLE PROPHECY! And you can prove it. But will you believe God? Or will you wait until it is too late physically to even respond to God? If not for divine intervention, the human race would face extinction! We live in a time of *no more delay and are racing* toward that prophetic fulfillment!

Meanwhile, Americans pick up the remote and flip channels to see who is playing on ESPN. AS THEY DISTRACT THEMSELVES, THIS WORLD IS ABOUT TO EXPLODE! MAN IS ABOUT TO SET THE WORLD ON FIRE!

Can't we see that there is no human solution to this crisis? Matthew 24:21-22 tell us exactly that. Without the return of Jesus Christ, mankind would war all the way to the point that there would not be a single human being left alive on Earth! This is talking about the nuclear world war just ahead of us!

But these verses also show that there is good news: Jesus Christ is going to stop us from destroying ourselves completely! He—not an Islamic Mahdi currently hiding in a well—is going to return to this Earth. Jesus Christ is going to return in all power from heaven and place His feet upon the Mount of Olives, and bring us the real, true and lasting peace that we all desire!

## 'Because of Transgression'

Satan the devil is working to tear down the United States. That is his goal. He and the demons have been cast down to Earth; they know they have only a short time left, and they are full of wrath (Revelation 12:12).

A technique that the devil has used time and again throughout history is to empower a leader who is able to do his damage from within.

Why would God allow this to happen to the U.S.? God does not put the primary blame on a political leader, the way that so many commentators tend to do.

One of the Bible's prophecies of this calamity explains the reason why this destructive leader is able to come to power. It is a prophecy of a time when this happened within the Church of God to destroy it from within, but the same principle applied to the United States in this end time. This prophecy in Daniel 8:12 reveals that this individual was empowered to do his destructive work "by reason of TRANSGRESSION, and it cast down the truth to the ground; and it practised, and prospered." This prophecy is explained in *America Under Attack.*

God allowed this attack "by reason of transgression"—because of the TERRIBLE SINS OF THE PEOPLE OF AMERICA!

The U.S. has sinned and turned away from God about as far as it possibly could.

As explained in *The United States and Britain in Prophecy,* America has a history with God. It has received wonderful blessings from God. Yet look at how our nation is living today. God says we have become like wicked Sodom and Gomorrah! (Isaiah 1:10). He is DISGUSTED with our morals and our spiritual lives! The nation's conduct has gotten so bad that GOD SAYS, *EVEN WHEN YOU LIFT UP YOUR HANDS AND PRAY TO ME, I WILL NOT*

*ANSWER YOU!* (verse 15). He is talking to America! He warns that our cities are going to burn with fire (verse 7), but if we wait until the last minute, when we ask for His help, He will refuse!

The superpower America is going to fall. It will drag down our closest allies, the British peoples (including Canada, Australia, New Zealand) and the Jewish nation.

All of this is happening because of transgression. When we are caught up in sin, God will not protect us against the devil—and we don't stand a chance against him and his demons without God's protection. Satan is simply too powerful.

Though in many ways it is the leaders who are drawing this nation to its death, the people deserve the blame most of all. God *allows* it to happen, and HE BLAMES—not one individual at the top—but THE *PEOPLE* WHO ARE TRANSGRESSING.

We must see what is happening in America today as God does. We have to recognize the cause and see the spiritual dimension. Then we can look at Bible prophecy and see exactly where it is leading. It is far more serious than the vast majority of people recognize.

But in the end, these nation-destroying disasters are actually *correction from God* to help us see our sins and repent of them. The same Bible that prophesies of our cities burning shows that, ultimately, all the suffering will help bring this nation to its senses and prepare us to submit to God once Jesus Christ returns to this Earth. Thank God for that!

The only solution to our massive problems is repentance toward God (Ezekiel 33:11). God will protect nations or individuals who repent now—*before* the great and dreadful Day of the Lord.

Satan's growing wrath against the nations of Israel as his time grows shorter will climax in the worst suffering in human history—a period the Bible calls the Great Tribulation. After 2½ years of tribulation, the Day of the Lord will begin, a full year of God's punishment on the nations.

The good news, though, is revealed right there in the very same prophecies that explain these events to us. Right after the Day of the Lord, at last will come the Second Coming of Jesus Christ to solve *all* these problems *forever!* In Daniel 8:23-25, when it speaks of the Satan-inspired political Antiochus leading the Holy Roman Empire, it gives this stirring conclusion: "[H]e shall magnify himself in his heart, and by peace shall destroy many: he shall also stand up against the Prince of princes"—that is JESUS CHRIST! Inspired by the devil, this evil man will actually try to take on Christ Himself! And what will be the outcome? "[H]e shall be broken without hand"—that is, broken BY THE POWER OF GOD!

The events we see unfolding are deeply sobering. But they should also fill us with hope—and anticipation of the great event they lead DIRECTLY into: the Second Coming of Christ to this Earth!

Once Christ banishes the devil and takes His rightful place on the throne over the Earth, we will have joy and happiness and peace for the rest of eternity! Thank God for that!

SEVEN

# Incredible 'Hope in Your End'

THESE ARE DARK DAYS FOR AMERICA. AND IF YOU understand the prophecies of the Bible, you know that they are about to get a lot darker. But it is crucial that we see the bad news in the larger context. God is allowing these crises because such punishment is necessary before He can really begin to bless our people—as He deeply desires and fully intends to do!

The same Bible that prophesies of the curses befalling us also foretells of the ultimate, super-inspiring outcome!

Here is an excerpt from our booklet *The Wonderful World Tomorrow—What It Will Be Like,* written by Herbert W. Armstrong (request your free copy):

## How Utopia Will Come!

But now let's be specific.

Let's see just how tomorrow's utopia is to be ushered in. Remember, this wonderful world-state will not be achieved all at once.

Every major step of these soon-coming events is laid bare before our eyes in biblical prophecy.

The same Jesus Christ who walked over the hills and valleys of the Holy Land and the streets of Jerusalem more than 1,900 years ago is coming again. He said He would come again. After He was crucified, God raised Him from the dead after three days and three nights (Matthew 12:40; Acts 2:32; 1 Corinthians 15:3-4). He ascended to the throne of God, headquarters of the government of the universe (Acts 1:9-11; Hebrews 1:3; 8:1; 10:12; Revelation 3:21).

He is the "nobleman" of the parable, who went to the throne of God—the "far country"—to be coronated as King of kings over all nations, and then to return to Earth (Luke 19:12-27).

Again, He is in heaven until the "times of restitution of all things" (Acts 3:19-21). *Restitution* means restoring to a former state or condition. In this case, the restoring of God's government on Earth, and thus, the restoring of world peace, and utopian conditions.

Present world turmoil, escalating wars and contentions will climax in world trouble so great that, unless God intervenes, no human flesh would be saved alive (Matthew 24:22). At its very climax when delay would result in blasting all life from off this planet, Jesus Christ will return. This time He is coming as divine God. He is coming in all the power and glory of the universe-ruling Creator (Matthew 24:30; 25:31). He is coming as "King of kings, and Lord of lords" (Revelation 19:16), to establish world super-government and rule all nations "with a rod of iron" (Revelation 19:15; 12:5).

Think of it. The glorified Christ—coming in all the splendor, the supernatural power and the glory of God Almighty—coming to save mankind alive—coming to stop escalating wars, nuclear mass destruction, human pain and suffering—coming to usher in peace, abundant well-being, happiness and joy for all mankind. …

World-famous scientists now say frankly that the *only* hope for survival on Earth is a supreme world-ruling government, controlling all military power. They admit that is impossible for man to accomplish. Christ is coming to give us just that. …

A leading American newsweekly gave the following surprising appraisal of man's *only hope:* The once optimistic hope of Americans, the article said, for a well-ordered and stable world, is fading. Expenditures close to a trillion dollars have failed to provide stability. Rather conditions have worsened. This appraisal indicated that among officials, the prevailing view is gaining acceptance that tensions and world problems are becoming too deep-seated to be solved "except by a strong hand from someplace." [This was written in 1966!]

"A strong hand from someplace." God Almighty is going to send a very strong hand from "someplace" to save humanity!

Notice this hope-filled promise from God through the Prophet Jeremiah: "Thus saith the LORD; Refrain thy voice from weeping, and thine eyes from tears: for thy work shall be rewarded, saith the LORD; and they shall come again from the land of the enemy. And THERE IS HOPE IN THINE END, saith the LORD, that thy children shall come again to their own border" (Jeremiah 31:16-17).

God *promises* that there is real HOPE in America's END! The same Bible that prophesied America's fall also prophesies that its brightest days are *yet to come!*

If you really believe these prophecies, you will understand why no politician can make America "great again." Only God can do that—and it has to be done *His way.* But He has given us ironclad promises that He absolutely WILL DO SO!

When God chose the biblical nation of Israel, He intended it to be an example and a blessing to ALL nations, leading them into a relationship with Him (read passages like Deuteronomy 4:5-8). Though that nation failed, the goal that God had for Israel anciently is still one He intends to accomplish. God *still* wants Israel's descendants to fulfill the glorious purpose of serving as a shining example to the world! And one day soon, THEY WILL BE!

Look at verses 6 and 7 of Jeremiah 31, which is a prophecy of the world after Jesus Christ returns. Verse 6 is about *Ephraim,* which is the prophetic name God has given to Great Britain. Verse 7 is about Jacob—a prophetic name for America and Britain—which it calls "THE CHIEF OF THE NATIONS." In other words, these will be the *leading nations* in the World Tomorrow!

This chapter pictures God lovingly gathering all people from these nations (verses 8-10), showering them with blessings (verses 12-17), and establishing His New Covenant with them (verses 31-34).

Jeremiah 33 also depicts the time after America and Britain have endured the Tribulation. God promises to restore prosperity to them and make them a positive example. They will become "A PRAISE AND AN HONOUR BEFORE ALL THE NATIONS OF THE EARTH, which shall hear all the good that I do unto them: and they shall fear and tremble for all the goodness and for all the prosperity that I procure unto it" (verse 9). Yes, people will be moved to worship God at His outpouring of generosity and love toward these nations!

It's hard to imagine how great America is going to be. But this much we know: AMERICA IS GOING TO BE GREAT AGAIN!

# TOMORROW'S NEWS TODAY!

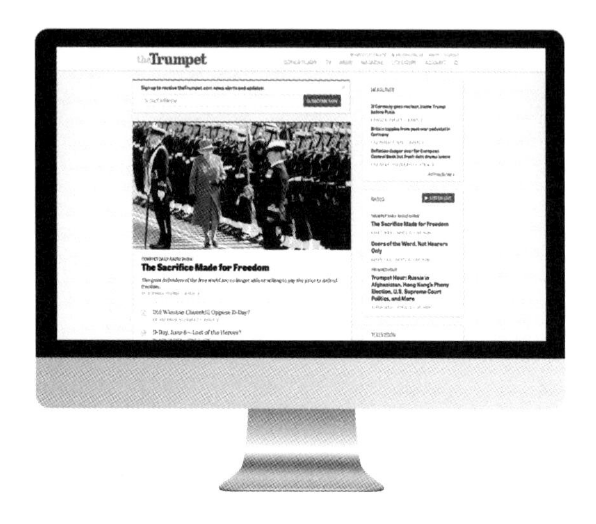


TheTrumpet.com closely tracks the news that fulfills Bible prophecy. If you want to see the prophecies of America discussed in *Great Again* come to pass on a daily basis, visit **theTrumpet.com**.

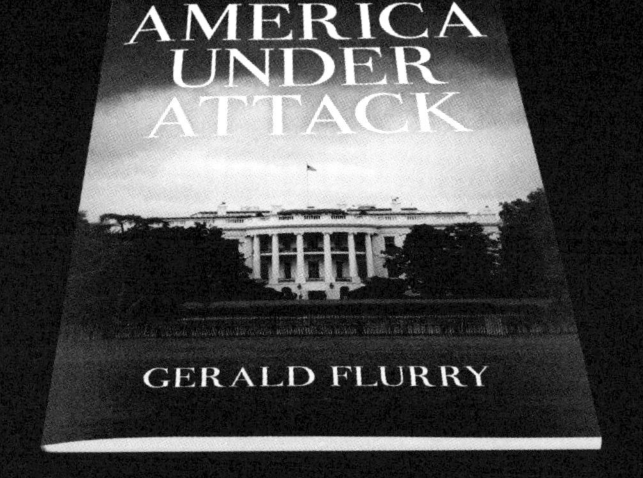


America's biggest threat is already inside its gates. To learn what it is, request your free copy of Gerald Flurry's booklet ***America Under Attack***.

Get the best news analysis in your hands by subscribing to your free subscription of the *Philadelphia Trumpet* newsmagazine.

Get ***10 FREE*** issues each year, already paid for and ready to be mailed to you.

**ONLINE:** *theTrumpet.com/literature/trumpet_magazine*

# Does God exist?

Many assume they know the answer, but how many actually prove it? Do you simply believe what you were taught from childhood?

To prove this question for yourself, request your free copy of Herbert W. Armstrong's ***Does God Exist?***

# Can you prove it?

God boldly states His Word is truth, but have you proved the Bible is the authoritative Word of the Creator?

You need to know—after all, if the Bible is the inspired Word of God you will be judged by it. Request your free copy of Herbert W. Armstrong's ***The Proof of the Bible***.

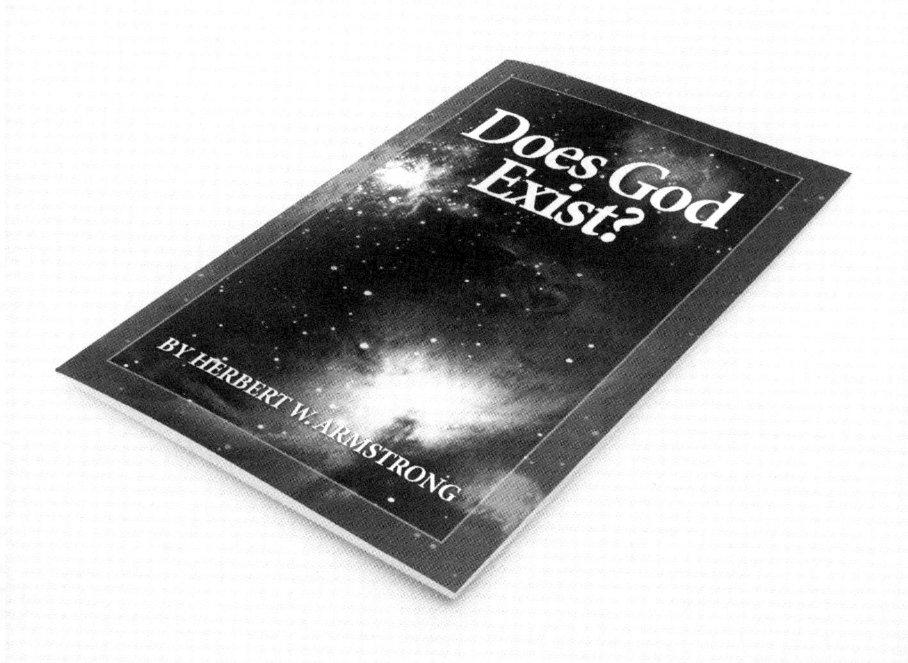

# You Can Understand the Bible!

BELIEVE IT OR NOT, THE BIBLE WAS WRITTEN FOR OUR day—this generation! No book is as up to date as the Bible. It explains the causes of present world conditions; it reveals what is ahead in the next few years. In its pages are the solutions to every problem we face in life—from personal and family relationships to national economics and foreign policy.

Yet ironically, this incredible book is the least understood of all books. Most people, when they try to read it, find that they simply cannot understand it. Many assume it is irrelevant and out-of-date for our modern age.

But you can understand the Bible!

Herbert W. Armstrong College has been helping thousands to learn both the meaning of current events and the true purpose of life through the *Herbert W. Armstrong College Bible Correspondence Course*. Over

**Enroll in the *Herbert W. Armstrong College Bible Correspondence Course***

*bcc.hwacollege.org*

letters@pcog.org

1-800-772-8577 (toll-free)

PCG | P.O. Box 3700 | Edmond, OK 73083

NO CHARGES. NO FOLLOW-UP. NO OBLIGATION.

100,000 students from around the world have enrolled in this unique, 36-lesson course of biblical understanding.

This course has been designed to guide you through a systematic study of your own Bible. The Bible is the only textbook. Best of all, these lessons are absolutely free. There is no cost or obligation—ever.

Sign up online and automatically receive your first four lessons along with a test. You will unlock four more lessons after passing each periodic test. If you would rather receive the lessons by mail, call to receive them free.

Why delay? Begin to understand your Bible today! Simply call, visit us online or write to the address nearest you and ask to be enrolled in the *Herbert W. Armstrong College Bible Correspondence Course*.

Join over 100,000 who have already enrolled in this free Bible course, and begin to really understand your entire Bible for the first time!

# Can you find America mentioned in the Bible?

To fully understand why America is declining, you first have to understand who America is.

To receive a detailed study and proof of America's identity in Bible prophecy, request your free copy of Herbert W. Armstrong's book ***The United States and Britain in Prophecy***.

## CONTACT INFORMATION

To reach the Philadelphia Church of God to order literature or to request a visit from one of God's ministers:

### MAILING ADDRESSES WORLDWIDE

**UNITED STATES:** Philadelphia Church of God
P.O. Box 3700, Edmond, OK 73083

**CANADA:** Philadelphia Church of God
P.O. Box 400, Campbellville, ON L0P 1B0

**CARIBBEAN:** Philadelphia Church of God
P.O. Box 2237, Chaguanas, Trinidad, W.I.

**BRITAIN, EUROPE AND MIDDLE EAST:**
Philadelphia Church of God, P.O. Box 16945
Henley-in-Arden, B95 8BH, United Kingdom

**AFRICA:** Philadelphia Church of God
Postnet Box 219, Private Bag X10010, Edenvale, 1610

**AUSTRALIA, THE PACIFIC ISLES, INDIA AND SRI LANKA:**
Philadelphia Church of God
P.O. Box 293, Archerfield, QLD 4108, Australia

**NEW ZEALAND:** Philadelphia Church of God
P.O. Box 6088, Glenview, Hamilton 3246

**PHILIPPINES:** Philadelphia Church of God
P.O. Box 52143, Angeles City Post Office, 2009 Pampanga

**LATIN AMERICA:** Philadelphia Church of God, Attn: Spanish Department
P.O. Box 3700, Edmond, OK 73083 United States

### WEBSITES

**PHILADELPHIA CHURCH OF GOD:** www.pcog.org
**THE TRUMPET:** theTrumpet.com
**ARMSTRONG INTERNATIONAL CULTURAL FOUNDATION:** ArmstrongAuditorium.org
**HERBERT W. ARMSTRONG COLLEGE:** HWACollege.org

### CONNECT WITH US

**EMAIL:** letters@pcog.org
**FACEBOOK:** facebook.com/PhiladelphiaChurchofGod
**TWITTER:** @PCG_News